CRYSTAL HEALING

Applying the Therapeutic Properties of Crystals and Stones

Volume II

First published in 1987 by:
Aurora Press
205 Third Avenue, Suite 2A
New York, N.Y. 10003

ISBN: 0--943358-30-2
Library of Congress Catalogue No: 86-071635

Cover Photo
© Gail Russell, 1987
Box 241
Taos, N.M. 87571

CRYSTAL HEALING

Applying the
Therapeutic Properties
of
Crystals and Stones

VOLUME II

KATRINA RAPHAELL

AURORA PRESS

205 Third Avenue   2A   New York, N.Y. 10003

TABLE OF CONTENTS

PART III
MISCELLANEOUS TIDBITS

ABOUT THE AUTHOR

Katrina Raphaell has extensively worked with New Age Healing Arts for over 16 years. Her professional experience includes: nursing, teaching and practicing massage therapies, and other related healing modalities. While Director of Health Care for a natural drug and alcohol rehabilitation center, she had the opportunity to apply her knowledge of nutrition, herbology, hydrotherapy, yoga, meditation technologies, kinesiology, flower essences, homeopathy and various forms of natural healing methods.

Through her studies and healing work, Katrina became increasingly aware of the mental and emotional imbalances associated with physical dis-ease. As the world of crystals opened up to her, Katrina was guided to use the energies of light and color to balance the more subtle aspects of our being—emotional, mental, subconscious and spiritual. Applying the information received in her personal meditations, she experienced first hand information, about how to utilize the light forces within the mineral kingdom to benefit oneself and others.

To bring this information to a wider audience, Katrina authored *Crystal Enlightenment* in 1985, which was the result of her personal study, work with clients and research. The material contained in her books, is part of a sacred knowledge, on how to use crystals and stones for healing and the expansion of consciousness. In order to facilitate the art of Crystal Healing, Ms. Raphaell opened the Crystal Academy of Advanced Healing Arts in Taos, New Mexico, making available intensive seminars, and courses for in depth studies. The Crystal Academy also encourages further gathering of information and research into the potential and as yet undiscovered qualities of crystals.

Nationally, Katrina is a popular lecturer, and with translations of her books in other languages, is invited to participate internationally in workshops and conferences.

PREFACE

The power of crystals is upon us and cannot be denied. They are used everywhere in the world today for many purposes. The memory chips, the very life of computers responsible for propelling us into the technological age are pure silicon dioxide: quartz. Ultrasound devices, oscillatives for controlling radio frequencies in electronic equipment, capacitators to modify energy capacity in circuits, transducers to transmit energy from one system to another, and condensors that store energy all depend upon quartz to function. Crystals and stones are without a doubt on the rise. Their ancient and futuristic powers are now, only after thousands of years, available for personal upliftment and planetary evolvement.

Until the year 1980 there was very little information concerning the esoteric and healing aspects of crystals and their former use in the root civilizations. Now abundant information on any aspect, from varied perspectives, on the power, potential, and use of crystals is available to thousands of people who are being instinctively drawn to use them in their own personal development and healing practices.

My advice to those in search of what they already inwardly know concerning crystals, is to use your own intuition as you explore the resources of this phenomenal world of light and acknowledge what rings true on your own inner touchstone. Information in *Crystal Enlightenment, Vol. I,* and the following material in *Crystal Healing, Vol. II,* is what I have personally received, experienced and witnessed in my work and research with crystals during the last decade. Your experience is your own. Personal unfoldment with crystals is dependent upon the willingness each individual has to sit, be still, clear the mind, open the heart, and perceive the insight that will be perfectly made to order.

Crystals and stones are pure manifestations in material form and varied color frequencies of light, demonstrating to us the reality of clarity, stability, beauty, divine law, and spiritual perfection. They are arriving on the scene in the nick of time to teach us how to activate and radiate the full potential of our own inner radiance. The crystals can serve as powerful tools in teaching us how to heal ourselves of the wounds of ancient lifetimes as they bring the mind into a state of peace in the present moment. Then, the power of the higher self can be consciously connected to the infinite spirit of creation from which springs forth all wealth, abundance and joy of heaven and earth.

The 1980's and the 1990's are major transition times in the history of the Earth. We are all in the process of transformation. The crystals and stones are very much a part of the personal and planetary initiations that are occurring and serving to accelerate our healing and

4

growth. The work that is now being done with crystals will continue to expand into every aspect of our lives and into rightful acknowledgment in the medical world. Even now crystals are being used in lasers in microscopic surgery. A century ago the concept of acupuncture and subtle energy pathways was balked at until its success rate proved its validity. Crystal healing has now been rebirthed and will, as destiny dictates, prove to be the most powerful method of healing not only for the body, but also in relieving ailments of the mind and heart which cause physical dis-ease.

As the light, color frequency, energy and radiance of crystals are infiltrated into the aura, the shadows of doubt are cleared from the mind, the bonds of fear are dissolved from the heart, and the body is then free to manifest a state of harmony with spirit. The Crystal Academy of Advanced Healing Arts is dedicated to the art and practice of crystal healing. The Academy is available to any sincere student wishing further training in the laying on of stones and associated therapeutic principals (see page 213).

Crystal Healing, Vol. II is designed to give the lay person as well as the professional adequate information to incorporate the power of crystals and stones into personal life or into a healing practice. Very specific advanced techniques and therapies are given which will enable one (with the prerequisite information in *Crystal Enlightenment, Vol. I*) to consciously contact the inner source of wisdom and access great quantities of light and energy to heal ourselves. This will enable true expression of the higher self to manifest in our lives.

What I find fascinating and extremely hopeful is that many people already subconsciously (or consciously) know about the power and potential of crystal healing. The memory veils from ancient days are being lifted as personal research and individual experience with crystals and stones is forming the foundation for true knowledge. It is inspiring that the light forces are being crystallized and materialized to be actively used in our lives for numerous purposes, from making our watches tick properly to healing the depths of our hearts.

The receptivity to the information in *Crystal Enlightenment, Vol. I* was a positive indication that many people identified with the body of knowledge presented and that together, we are growing closer to the light through the medium of crystals. Crystal power is increasing in force, and will continue to do so as we cross the threshold into the Golden Age of Knowing. In essence, crystals and stones are teachers and guides for us as they undoubtedly reflect and manifest the light which is the common denominator for all creation.

For me, crystals are the last rung on the long ladder of advanced healing arts. They are the final phase in the development of pure healing energy which results in what is commonly defined as "miracles." But it is very important to also realize when working with crystals, as beautiful and attractive as they are, that they are still just tools and to empower them to a greater degree than we empower ourselves is to lose sight of the real lesson. The crystals are not "it," the light is "it," we are "it"!! To effectively use crystals to their highest purpose is to learn and grow in our ability to use our own light and inner resources as an ultimate goal. Crystals are instruments of power that can successfully point us in the right direction to claim, develop, embrace and manifest the light within us that they so clearly reflect.

Preface

Crystal Healing, the second volume in this *Crystal Trilogy*, is dedicated to everyone who identifies with this information. It is for the crystal healers who are boldly stepping forth and for those who are in need of healing. It is for the children and the Earth. The information on the following pages remains forever open to the revision of higher truth as it unfolds through personal experience. It is my prayer and conscious projection that the knowledge contained herein will be used only for positive purpose, and that through it many people will be drawn closer to their own lighted center of truth and power. Thank you.

Katrina Raphaell

PART I

ADVANCED CRYSTAL HEALING PRACTICES

CHAPTER I

ADVANCED CRYSTAL HEALING PRACTICES

In *Volume I, Crystal Enlightenment*, the healing properties of many crystals and stones are given, as well as basic information on crystal healing techniques and various layouts of stones. Making this information available to people who would practically utilize it gave way to the growing sense of responsibility to also share the specific techniques that are used once the crystals and stones are laid on and powerful energies begin to flow. Many of you have already witnessed these effects. You might not have known what to do, or how to process the changes that inevitably will occur when the chakra centers are opened and whatever the blockage is, surfaces, ready to be released. Here it is—what to do, how to contact the source, gain spiritual perspective, understand the root causes of dis-ease and how to neutralize, learn the inherent lessons, let go, and move onward and upward.

The therapeutic approaches described herein are those that I have worked with and developed in many years of practicing crystal healing. Many of the therapeutics are, in and of themselves, complete systems of theory and practice (past life therapy, exorcism, etc.) They are used in this book in relationship to the art and practice of crystal healing. The effect of any therapy is increased and healing energy amplified when using crystals in conjunction with it. I would suggest further personal research into any areas one is not familiar with to incorporate a well rounded knowledge of the subjects. It is my privilege to present these techniques to you, and ask that you align yourself with your own inner light and the energies of the crystals and stones before you use them.

The art of performing crystal healing is a responsibility that needs to be consciously acknowledged and accepted before one embarks into practice with other people. Much damage can and has been done by those who were unaware of the power that is generated when crystals and stones blend with the human electromagnetic field. Many subtle and overt changes occur that one needs to be prepared for and capable of dealing with. The aura, when infused with light reflected off of the stones, will have a direct effect on every other aspect of being. Mental awareness is elevated, the emotional body becomes hyper-sensitive, and if the proper procedures are applied, spiritual energy can be integrated into the physical body and miraculous healing can occur. If unaware and naive about the forces that are being dealt with, severe disassociation, psychic vulnerability and unchanneled energies could create more harm than good. With the specific therapeutic techniques described on the following pages, the power of crystals and stones can be harnessed and their energies used for healing and upliftment.

Crystal healing is a progressive art, one that has the potential to create complete healing, inclusive of the mental, emotional, physical, and spiritual bodies. Practicing crystal healing is an opportunity to let go and let God. It is the time when the heart listens to the messages of the soul, a time to plunge deeply into trust in the inner self. Crystal healing is dedicated to the highest energies of light and color as they act upon the subtle levels of the human being. When this energy interaction takes place, the deepest essence of a person can be accessed. It then becomes possible to see why we have created the realities that we have in our lives. When we understand why we have attracted our circumstances and what the invaluable spiritual lessons are inherent in our life's events, we can then take complete responsibility for ourselves and create our lives the way we choose. Peace and personal empowerment are the natural way of being to one who is in harmony with the self and understands the sometimes hidden purpose behind why events happen in life the way that they do. It is then no longer necessary to play the role of victim, of the controlled, the powerless, and the prisoner of life.

The art of giving a crystal healing requires constant mental focus and an ability to let go of one's personal problems in order to completely tune into the person that is being worked with. When receiving a crystal healing, the blockages in the mental or emotional bodies will be surfaced into the conscious mind in order to be viewed from an expanded perspective. Crystal healings are designed to bring more light force and color into the aura as natural light reflects off of the stones and energy is amplified. This facilitates clearer vision into the miasmas and personal karmic patterns that can govern life events. With this insight it is possible to consciously gain understanding, complete cycles, clear karma, learn invaluable lessons, and come into complete personal empowerment.

The crystals and stones that are laid on the vital centers of the body reflect and generate forces that infuse the aura with light. With the aura open and clear, the chakra centers are activated and conscious contact with the deepest, purest aspects of the self can be made. As the vibrational frequency of the aura raises, whatever mental, emotional, or subconscious energies are vibrating at a lower frequency will surface into the mind and heart to be cleansed, healed, and transformed. With the increased light and healing vibrations of the stones combined with the described therapies in this book, it is possible to positively transform the self image. By changing outdated belief systems and revising concepts and attitudes about life, inner harmony and peace can result. With personal peace as the foundation, the contentment that we carry within our own hearts will serve to transform the planet and the physical world will reflect and manifest our internal state of being.

CHAPTER II

PREPARATION

Before beginning a crystal healing it is important to clear your mind, center yourself, and focus attention within and on the crystals and stones that you will be working with. Before your client arrives sit down with your stones in front of you and breathe deep and long. You may want to hold in your left hand an Amethyst crystal that would aid in the power of intuition or you might choose to place your favorite personal meditation crystal to your third eye or heart center. Allow the mind to follow the flow of the breath and with each exhale release any of your own concerns or problems, visually drawing more light and energy into your consciousness and body on the inhale. Call upon any personal sources of healing power as you prepare to align with your client and work with the power of the stones. A decree that I personally affirm before beginning crystal healings is this:

"I call upon the Light of the Great White Brotherhood.
I call upon the Light of the Great Central Sun.
I call upon the Light of my own Eternal Being.
I call upon the Light of the Infinite One."

Having repeated this affirmation at least three times, I feel cleared and prepared to begin. (This is also a prayer for strength and protection that can be used at any time.)

Centering and aligning yourself in this way before you begin not only prepares you to work with the forces at hand, but also assists your own ability to release your personal concerns in order to be consciously present with the circumstances at hand. It is an ideal opportunity to be in a state of active meditation and increase your ability to remain clear, perceptive, and aware while in a state of physical action.

PREPARING THE ENVIRONMENT

Before and after each crystal healing session, it is important to not only cleanse and recharge the crystals and stones that are used, but to also clear the air of any psychic debris that may be lurking in the environment. There are several ways to accomplish this. One of the best is to open the windows and doors and let fresh air circulate. Another effective method is to light incense or smudge sticks, which are cedar and sage sticks, most commonly known in the native American Indian tradition (see More Cleansing and Recharging Techniques, page 173). Also, candles can be lit and burned for at least ten minutes. Equally effective is a crystal meditation where the termination of a Clear Quartz generator is directed out from

16

the third eye with the conscious projection in mind of attracting fresh vibrant energy and dissolving any negative thoughts or feelings that may have lingered from previous healings. The importance of a positive environment will assist you, the healer, to stay neutral and centered, as well as providing for the recipient a safe clear place in which transformation can occur.

Another important factor to be aware of is that the person you are working with will more than likely be going through changes and clearing emotions, releasing old thoughts, and discharging negative energies. As a healer it is important to protect yourself so that you don't take that energy into your aura and on into your personal life. One of the best ways to protect yourself is by holding your favorite meditation crystal (Clear Quartz generator) with the termination pointing out away from you while performing the therapeutics of the healing.

During your personal preparation time set a mental image of light entering into you through the crown chakra on the inhale and radiating out from the heart center to surround you in a field of protective white light on the exhale. This will increase the healing energy emanating from your heart chakra. It is also important to ground yourself while performing the healing and working with crystals and stones. To do this, visualize light (or rich colors) traveling from the crown to the base of the spine on the inhale. On the exhale, direct the energy down through the legs and into the earth through the soles of the feet. With these images preset it will be possible to maintain the protective effects throughout the healing. Never set up an image of inhaling energy in from the recipient and exhaling out through the top of your head, as this will increase your vulnerability to negative energies being discharged and can result in physical dehabilitation and/or psychic exhaustion. Awareness and a positive approach will secure a peaceful setting for the protection of the practitioner and the well being of the client.

The environment in which crystal healings are performed should be quiet with a minimum amount of outside noise, conducive to relaxation and meditation. If living in environments where quiet space is limited (or if you travel out to people's homes), it may be necessary to create a protective field in the area where the healing will be performed. This can be done by placing a Clear Quartz generator in each corner with the terminations pointing towards the center of the room. Then stand in the middle of the room and hold a Clear Quartz generator in the right hand with the termination alternately pointing towards each of the other crystals. As you direct your healing energy through the crystal you are holding, and rotate in a counterclockwise direction, you will seal the room against intrusive outside influences (Laser Wands may also be used in these circumstances to create a protective force field, see page 143).

Daytime, with the sun's natural light reflection off of the stones, is ideal. It is beneficial to have soft mellow music in the background and to have as many crystals present as possible to aid in the expansion of the light force. A massage table or a table about waist height is best to use. The recipient should lie face up while receiving the healing. Two pillows are used, one under the head and the other under the knees to prevent lower back stress.

To get the full effect it is best to place the stones upon bare skin, so it is optimal to be naked from at least the waist up. If this is not a comfortable situation for the recipient, natural fibers (cotton, wool, silk) should be

18

worn to facilitate energy conduction of the stones. If the environment is cool, a blanket should be used to cover and warm the feet, legs, and arms as the torso is exposed to the elements. Crystal healings often take up to two hours and it is important that the recipient remain comfortable and relaxed. It will often seem to the receiver that only a short time has passed because they have gone so deep within. The linear time frequencies that we experience in the normal waking state are drastically altered when high vibrational light forces from the crystals and stones are infused into the auric field. This time warp phenomenon is common and needs to be monitored by the healer, concluding the healing when you receive the intuitive inclination to do so. During this time the crystal healer is responsible for the comfort and the well being of the person being worked with. If a person feels physically safe and taken care of, it will be much easier to connect with the deeper realms of being.

Along with the physical security, it is just as important to create an even deeper sense of trust with the person that you are working with. Very profound intimate levels are being accessed during crystal healings, sometimes deeper than a person has ever experienced before. Often thoughts or memories will surface that are very personal or potentially embarrassing. It is very important to maintain an attitude of nonjudgment and to keep all that is revealed confidential. Trust and confidentiality are key attributes that will insure a positive emotional environment for healing to occur.

When your client arrives sit down and through open conversation discover what needs to be worked on, where blockage or constriction exists, what part of the physical body is imbalanced or dis-eased, and what is happening on a personal level. Ask the individual what needs to be focused on and cleared. This conversation is the first indication to you, the crystal healer, where to concentrate and what stones to use.

Usually the person who is drawn to receive a crystal healing inwardly knows what changes need to occur in order to change, grow and heal. Crystal healings are designed to allow the recipient to consciously access depths of being previously unavailable, and draw upon personal resources to answer all questions and heal any wound.

PRESENT TIME CONSCIOUSNESS

Giving or receiving a crystal healing is an act of meditation. It is a time to let go of everything but the reality of the present moment. It is from the awareness of the "now" that we can contact the inner source and access accurate information to gain knowledge concerning any issue at hand. The solutions to the great riddles of the universe lie within us. By extracting the distilled essence of the eternal moment we can have access to answers about our past karmas, present circumstances, and future events. All time exists in the neutral zone of the moment. When the mind becomes stilled and focused within, it is then possible to see with the all-encompassing vision of the third eye and know the truth about oneself and the universe of which we are a part.

It is important for the person who is giving the crystal healing to remain very aware and in the moment, not having thoughts drifting in and out of personal circumstances. It is essential to stay attuned to the person who is receiving the healing, to monitor the breath and watch for signs of release. It is a time to be very aware of the crystals and stones that are being used, placing and removing them as needed. Even though you will be using your intellectual knowledge of the stones, the chakra centers, color, etc., the foundation for awareness and action is based in the intuition, the knowing of the moment. With the mind stilled and consciousness stabilized in the present moment, it will be possible to follow the subtle impulses that the intuition will relay to direct the laying on and removal of stones, the personalized direction you give, and your individual attuned response to the person you are working with.

The person who is receiving the crystal healing has the unique opportunity to contact the very essence of being. Communion with the soul can occur when the mind is quiet and settled into the present moment and attention is turned within. Present time awareness is the initial key to dissolve the shadows of the subconscious, unlock the doors to the superconscious and cross the threshold into the realm of spirit. When this occurs it is possible to view dis-ease or imbalance with greater perspective, understanding from our experiences the evolutional growth achieved from even the most traumatic events. Full personal responsibility and empowerment is the first step in contributing to planetary upliftment. It starts in the present moment in conscious communion with our own infinite spark.

THE POWER OF THE BREATH

The breath is the main source of life energy that is available to human beings. Through the breath life force is taken into the body. From this vital exchange of gases each individual has a personal interaction with the universe. On the inhale we receive life energy, and on the exhale we give it back. We can live for long amounts of time without food and for days without water, but only for a few minutes without the precious life force that is received with each breath. It is this force that activates the chakra centers, revitalizes the subtle and physical bodies, and brings healing energy in to be utilized by conscious attunement and direction.

Becoming aware of the breath is one of the most effective ways of tuning into the moment. The breath exists in a state of constant presence. By attuning the mental focus to the breath the mind neutralizes and the intuition can be clearly acknowledged.

While lying face up on the table, eyes closed, verbally guide your client to be aware of each inhalation and each exhalation. Use images and visualizations to direct the mind inward. Keep your voice soft and melodious as you verbally direct the person's attention inward. Use images such as,

> *"Inhale and allow yourself to go deeply within, exhale and let go of any troubles, concerns or worries. Inhale and sink deeper into the center of yourself, exhale and surrender, relax, let go."*

Often it will be difficult for a person to breathe completely. Most people breathe only with their upper lungs. The reason for this being, when we fully and consciously breathe we experience the maximum stimulus in life, we take in completely. As we have grown up and been exposed to situations and circumstances that have been traumatic or painful, we often do not want to feel these experiences and subconsciously cut off the life force by breathing less air. When these events occur we shut down our breathing, because to breathe is to live, and life is not always pleasant or easy to assimilate. By cutting the breath short and shallow, we take in less life, experience less distress, less pain.

The trouble with this is that the subconscious memories and correlating emotions of each trauma are stored in the solar plexus where the breath refused to go. This creates a major blockage between the lower centers apexing at the navel and the upper chakras with the foundation at the heart. With energy constriction at the solar plexus it is impossible to completely integrate the powers of the heavens with the realities of the earth. Had we been able to stay focused and centered through each emotional shock, it would have been possible to breathe deeply and completely and in so doing stay relaxed and learn the lessons involved in life events. Since we are often unable to do this it becomes necessary to decharge the suppressed feelings at the solar plexus and release the old memories from the subconscious mind in order to heal the physical body and balance the upper and lower energy centers.

By observing the person's breath during crystal healings you can notice where they have stopped taking in life force. These are often areas that have become dis-eased and imbalanced. These are the areas that crystals and stones are often placed over, where you can work in the aura with a Clear Quartz generator crystal (see *Crystal Enlightenment, Vol. I*, pages 38–39), and where you will direct the conscious flow of the breath.

CENTER LINE FOCUS

One of the best techniques for tuning into the moment with the breath is called Center Line Focus. Begin by having the recipient close the eyes and focus on the breath. Visualizing a golden ball of light six inches above the top of the head, direct your client to draw this light in through the crown chakra and down into the center of the forehead, stimulating the third eye, and through each energy center all the way down to the base of the spine. It is of added benefit to touch each one of the chakra points as you verbally guide the flow of the breath through the center line. On the exhale the visualization is of the light traveling up the spine and out the top of the head. This conscious focus of light traveling up and down the spine allows one to mentally create a central golden cord which will channel the infinite light from above the crown into each chakra, integrating the power of spirit into mind, heart and body.

This center line focus is extremely valuable in stimulating the nervous system by concentrating on the central spinal cord, aligning the chakras by focusing on the shushumna (the etheric spine), and activating the meridian system by attuning to the governing and conception vessels.

Conscious breathing through the center line also allows identification with the neutral self and brings the mind and heart into a state of detachment. Again, verbally direct your client to:

Preparation

*"Inhale deeply through your center line, exhale
and release any thoughts as you focus on the light
moving through your spine. Inhale and go deeper
into your own radiant center, exhale and let go of
any tensions that may prevent you from going in
even deeper on the following inhale."*

Some people find it easier to inhale up the spine and
exhale down it. Do whatever works best for each individual. In circumstances where your client is not very
grounded (too mental, emotional or spacey) it would be
advantageous to direct the energy differently. You could
have them inhale and channel energy to the base of the
spine. On the exhale the visualization would be through
the anus or down the legs and through the soles of the
feet. The manner in which you direct the mental focus of
energy is based upon the needs of each individual and
could vary from treatment to treatment.

As the recipient relaxes, guide the breath into and
through the center line, using the diaphragm and the
abdominal muscles. It is important that the breath move
through the solar plexus and into the navel center. The
bridging of the heart chakra with the lower triangle of
energy is essential in order to integrate the healing energies of the stones directly into the physical body. The
navel is the center of the physical body and the heart
forms the base for the spiritual bodies. As golden light is
brought down the center line through the crown chakra
and deeply breathed into the navel, energy is transmitted
into the body for physical healing.

Once the recipient's breath is deep and complete, the
stones are placed upon the body. Throughout the healing,
use the Center Line Focus to keep your client in tune with
the life force and the power to personally channel energy.

25

Crystal Healing

As you proceed through the healing and your client becomes aware of suppressed emotions or mental images surface, it is most important to keep the breath deep and complete. The shortening or shallowing of the breath is the first indication that a person is getting in touch with the deeper psychological and emotional traumas that can be responsible for creating physical dis-ease. As you deal with these imbalances, it is often necessary to refocus on the breath and revisualize the center line in order to decharge and neutralize whatever debris is surfacing.

It is also helpful to actually lay your hands on the areas that are constricted and direct your client to breathe deeply into them. The laying on of hands is an ideal opportunity to direct healing energy through the power of touch into a troubled area. It also facilitates a recon- nection with parts of the body that may have been sub- consciously disassociated with.

If a person comes to you with stomach ulcers and during the crystal healing becomes aware of all of the fear and anxiety that was experienced as a child (that has been carried over into adult life), assist your client to breathe in and visualize a calming blue color into the stomach and diaphragm area, exhaling the fears and tensions. In this case the color blue is the antidote for the angry red ulcer- ation that has manifested. It would be of added benefit to place light blue stones over the stomach and solar plexus area (Turquoise, Gem Silica, Chrysocolla, Aquamarine, or Amazonite) as well as placing your hands over the area. Verbally direct conscious breathing, inhaling through the center line and exhaling tension out of the stomach area. It is of added benefit to work on or above distressed areas with a Clear Quartz generator crystal as you consciously project your healing energy through the crystal to be intensified and magnified.

26

Preparation

Throughout the healing and in personal private practice, the breath is the main tool for conscious attunement and empowerment.

To summarize: Each breath should be deep and complete, taking the life force throughout the body, particularly into areas that are troubled. Visualize the breath moving through the center line, coming down from the crown on the inhale and rising up from the base of the spine on the exhale. With each breath the navel area and abdominal muscles should expand and contract as the life force is integrated into the physical systems through the navel center. Use visualizations to guide and direct the breath into areas of distress, recharging with each inhale and releasing stress and tension with each exhale. See the lungs being filled as if you were filling a glass with water. On the inhale first the bottom is filled, then the middle, and finally the upper part of the lungs as the diaphragm descends and the abdominal muscles expand. To exhale the glass is emptied, from the top first, then the middle, contracting the abdominal muscles to push the breath up and out. This simple proper breathing technique can then be incorporated into an exercise that your client extends into a personal maintenance plan to continue circulating healing energy.

Most of us have never learned to breathe properly, to develop our vital exchange with the universe. Athletes, singers, yogis, and dancers have all learned to use their breath to increase personal vitality. The breath is power, and can be visualized and directed for healing. Anytime you need to focus, close your eyes, feel the power of the breath on the inhale, and release stress, pain, emotion or anxiety on the exhale. It is always there. It's yours to use.

STONE PLACEMENT

In Chapter III of *Crystal Enlightenment* six crystal healing layouts are suggested for your use. Any of these can be used, as well as any other creation that unfolds itself. Even though you will be using your knowledge of the chakras, the effects of color and the power of the stones, the actual stone placement is always an intuitive response to the moment and to the person that you are working with. There were times when I would anticipate a layout that I intended on doing before my client arrived. But when the time came to actually place the stones, the moment dictated a different combination than my expectation. I learned that even though you can intellectually anticipate, the clearest guidance is to follow your intuition for direction at each moment. If you open your heart, relax, and allow your mind to listen to the inner voice you will be correctly guided to the needed stone, where it is to be placed, why, and when it should be removed.

The manner in which you place stones to a large degree is determined by the person who is receiving the healing and how you want to direct the flow of energy. If someone is fearful, sorrowful, or lacking in self-love, you can focus around the heart chakra with Rose Quartz, pink and green Tourmaline, Green Aventurine, Kunzite, Rhodonite, Rhodochrosite, and other heart center stones. If someone is unable to activate the manifestation power that is needed to fulfill personal goals or feels depowered and helpless, you can work at the navel area with Citrine, Rutilated Quartz, Golden Topaz, Tiger's Eye, and Gold Calcite. If your client is unable to express what is felt, open the throat chakra with Gem Silica, Aquamarine, Blue Lace Agate, Amazonite and Chrysocolla. Even when focusing on a particular chakra it is important to

Preparation

place at least one stone at each of the other chakra points in order to balance the energy centers and integrate the effects throughout the system. For example: Place Smoky Quartz at the first center, Carnelian second chakra, Citrine at the navel, Green Aventurine at the solar plexus, Rose Quartz at the heart, Amazonite at the throat, Amethyst at the brow and Clear Quartz at the hairline.

Essentially stone placement is dependent upon the individual, the time, and your own attunement to the moment. The mandalas of color and design that are created in each individual layout are always different and specified to the unique circumstances at hand. It is an opportunity to be sensitively creative with the powers of light and color. Use your personal guidance and listen to the stones as they speak to your inner knowing.

Once the stones have been laid on and the recipient is aligning and attuning to their own lighted center (approximately fifteen minutes) is a very sensitive and vulnerable time. The crystal healer must be very attentive and aware, as a great influx of energy is being infiltrated into the aura and subsequently into the physical body. That is why deep breathing is so important—to integrate these most subtle energies into the physical systems. The entire metabolism readjusts to the increase of energy as the heart rate and blood pressure usually go up and can be noted by observing the throat and navel pulse. The recipient's awareness becomes extremely sensitized as the consciousness settles into the inner sanctums of the Self. It may be necessary at times (if a person is unable to integrate the higher energies of the stones into the aura) that some or all of the stones may need to be removed immediately. Once the breath is steadied and the pulse rate equalizes, then proceed with the healing.

PROTECTION AND GUIDANCE

The potential to activate high degrees of light force is unsurpassed during crystal healings when the frequencies of the stones blend with the human electromagnetic field. Inner realms can be accessed and the higher dimensions of reality become comprehensible. The threshold into the spiritual world is crossed as the crystals lighten the way. Essentially the aura is being opened and a person can become very vulnerable to psychic and etheric influences. You want only the highest and most positive forces and entities present. To insure this, hold the termination of a clear quartz generator out from your third eye as you affirm out loud a decree something like this:

> *"I call upon the highest powers of light and color to act upon and through the crystals and stones. I call upon (your client's name), master teachers and spiritual guides to be present with us and assist in this healing. Most importantly, I call upon the truest essence of (your client's name) to come forth and relay to his/her heart and mind whatever is needed at this time to gain understanding, clarity and healing."*

This statement is powerfully spoken to call upon protection and guidance. When completed, you can rest assured that only the most positive forces are present. It is also an invocation to your client's soul force to come forth to participate and communicate. Now, it is time to begin the therapy.

CHAPTER III
THE THERAPY

SOUL CONNECTION

Up until now the recipient has been passive while the crystal healer has verbally directed the consciousness inward while placing the stones on the body. Now it is time for interaction with the soul to occur and communication of that wisdom to be shared with the healer. At times, when the recipient is focused deep within the self, it may be hard to speak, but once verbal communication begins it usually continues without difficulty.

One of the most important aspects of the healing occurs now, conscious contact with the soul's presence. The main key to this communion is to recognize and acknowledge the subtle impressions as they surface from the soul level into the conscious mind. Often in our lives we receive these messages, but sometimes they go unnoticed or we hesitate to express them or follow the impulse through with attention or action. During a crystal healing, once the stones have been placed, the aura is cleared, and the recipient is relaxed and attuned within, whatever impressions are received are acknowledged and accepted as true without hesitation or doubt. Sometimes the images, impressions or symbols are vague, unfamiliar, or don't make sense. As you continue throughout the course of the healing it will all fall into order. It is the job of the crystal healer to assist in interpreting and defining the messages that will arise into the mind of the recipient. Conscious awareness of the present moment enables the healer to align with the soul level of the receiver and obtain intuitive guidance.

SOUL SYMBOL

Attention and conscious focus are the main keys to draw upon the inner knowing and activate the intuition. Having dedicated time to the internalization of awareness, we are now ready to actually integrate the wisdom from the soul level into the conscious mind. Having called upon protection and guidance, make a statement to the receptive mind of the receiver which will go something like this:

> *"With your mind very open, receptive and clear, we would now ask that the soul's presence give to your mind or your heart an image, symbol, vision, or sense of itself. As you become aware of this impression, please share with me what you perceive."*

This statement initiates the soul's presence into the healing. Work with whatever image arises in the mind at this time. Sometimes it will be an obvious symbol or sign.

Other times it will be colors or more abstract impressions. If you need to obtain clearer insight into the meaning, ask how the person feels about it, what it means, how it relates. One image that surfaced with a client of mine was of a toilet flushing. This didn't ring a bell to me, but upon asking what it meant to my client, he immediately knew that it was a sign of being ready to eliminate wastes or release debris that he no longer needed. This enabled us both to see that major cleansing was about to occur.

From this initial connection the healing evolves. If the symbol is the color green, symbolic of healing, you can direct the person to breathe green into problem areas and refer back to its healing essence as the session progresses. Once conscious contact with the soul level has been made, you can then direct attention into specific areas in need of healing, or into whatever issues your client wanted to focus on.

ALTERED VISION

With the conscious mind focusing within and the crystals lighting the way, a phenomenal world of understanding opens up. It is as if you can look at your life, your circumstances, and the universe from an entirely expanded perspective. From this point of view it is possible to see clearly the purpose behind events and understand why it was necessary to attract certain situations. At this level it is also possible to have access to your own akashic records as you review the recorded impressions of any event that has been experienced throughout your existence. The source of healing energy, with which all ailments can be cured, can be perceived and channeled by initiating altered vision.

As a crystal healer, your job is to guide your partner's attention to achieve inner knowing. Your voice should be soft, melodious and trusting. Through the power of your words, you guide, encourage, communicate and direct. If your voice is harmonious to the ear of the receiver you can facilitate your partner in accessing deeper states of awareness than would be possible without your assistance. The power of your words, when aligned with your own intuition, can initiate levels of consciousness similarly achieved through hypnotic trance. In some ways preliminary crystal healing techniques resemble hypnosis. The main difference is that the recipient remains totally conscious and in control throughout the session. In this way perspective and insight is achieved from the altered vision that is personally witnessed and experienced.

THE THIRD EYE AWAKENERS

There are several major stones that can be placed at the third eye center to initiate altered vision. They are Amethyst, Gem Silica, Azurite and Luvulite, all featured in *Crystal Enlightenment, Vol. I.* Each stone has its own special effect and can be used in combination with one another to create clear vision through which the soul can see with the third eye.

Amethyst is the main third eye stone that, like Rose Quartz for the heart, draws energy within for self healing and self illumination. Amethyst is the main meditation stone, serving to calm a troubled mind into a state of personal peace. The clear purple ray that Amethyst so perfectly reflects is like a shot of tranquility descending from the higher planes. Stilling the mind, Amethyst allows inner wisdom to be perceived.

A close friend to Amethyst and sharing in honor as one of the New Age stones is Her Highness, Gem Silica. She is often used in conjunction with Amethyst at the brow to stimulate the higher visionary powers, enabling the third eye to see beyond the illusions of time and space and into the realm of the spirit. Gem Silica introduces the vital blue green ray into the mind, awakening the inner senses to witness the wonders of the ethers. Gem Silica is the purest ray of blue, representing the feminine intuition that expresses the depth of a still blue mountain lake while simultaneously directing attention into the vast expanse of visionary space. Gem Silica is the main stone to use when working in the psychic arts to verbally transmit accurate perception when channeling, doing readings or counseling. Because blue is the natural color for the throat chakra, this stone can also be used directly on the throat points to facilitate the transference of visionary concepts into manifestation through the power of the spoken word. Gem Silica also lends her healing properties to the second chakra to ease conflicts arising from feminine identification, sexual friction or reproductive imbalances. Gem Silica is a multi-faceted stone in purpose and intrigue and can be used in crystal healing layouts in the various ways described. Evolving from Chrysocolla, there are many grades of quality that Gem Silica can express. The clearest pure grade should be used at the third eye center to insure accurate perception and interpretation of visionary experiences.

Azurite is the most powerful stone to use when consciously ready and prepared to meet personal fears straight on. Unlike Sodolite and Lapis, who trio Azurite in the Indigo Trinity, Azurite often crystallizes and in so doing has greater penetrative powers into the subconscious. Crystallization also creates greater light reflection, enabling Azurite to also dissolve the fears that surface that bind the mind in slavery to the past. Azurite should be used only when one is ready to look into the locked and blocked areas of the psyche. It is necessary for awareness to accompany use of this stone. Both the healer and the recipient should be aware of the powers of Azurite and be ready to deal with and process whatever will inevitably surface from the darkened areas of the subconscious. When pure Azurite wands are placed at the occiput area (base of the skull) unknown fears rooting back to the days of antiquity can be remembered and past life memories that are shrouded in fright can be recalled. It is best to use Azurite at the third eye point in conjunction with Amethyst to calm the mind and connect the consciousness to the inner self while processing the cause and effects of fear patterns. In partnership with Malachite at the solar plexus, which clears emotion, Azurite will be a thorough scourer of the mind, enabling a harmonious renewal of thought and feeling. When used with Gem Silica the deep indigo of Azurite is greatly aided by the clear sight of Mother Silica as the vision of the soul sees through fear tendencies to plant new seeds of thought.

Lord Luvulite was born onto this planet only a few years ago and now is daring to expose his pure regality in gem quality specimens. When Luvulite is used at the third eye center its clear mental understanding will relay to the mind exactly why the soul is attracting experiences and what lessons are to be learned. It is a perfect stone to use with its purple polarity, passive Amethyst, to ground into the mental realms of comprehension the wisdom of the soul. Luvulite is the male aspect of the purple ray as it ushers the intuitive knowing into the intellect for mental transformation and healing. With the combination of Azurite, Gem Silica and Luvulite at the third eye center, problems rooted in other lifetimes will be witnessed, purged, understood, and learned from. Luvulite is the main touchstone to use when knowledge into the source of physical dis-ease is ready to be revealed, worked with and healed.

These stones comprising the third eye quartet can be used interchangeably at the third eye center to still the mind, open inner vision, purify the thoughts attached to fear modes, and bring into understanding the soul's purpose behind all circumstance. These stones are very powerful in initiating altered vision. It is the responsibility of each person using these stones on other people to be aware of their individual effects. When using them, monitor your client's responses closely and observe the pulse rate, the rhythm of the breath and the subtle energy shifts. Direct the recipient's consciousness to the light in the center line and the smooth flow of the breath. As deeper relaxation and internalized focus occur the subtle responses of the inner self can be perceived.

*   *   *

There are many techniques that can be used to usher in altered vision. We will discuss a few of them. But remember, whatever comes through you with the individual circumstances, in the moment, with the intuitive forces at work, use as your guidance.

BODY OVERVIEW

This technique works best when there is a specific physical imbalance that is being worked with, but it is not limited to these situations. It can also be used to obtain a clear picture of potential physical dis-eases or to see the auric pattern. (This is also a good time for the healer to visually and mentally affirm your own protective field.) Direct your client to:

"Imagine yourself as if you were three feet above your body and looking down upon it. You can see inside the body to view the internal organs, the veins, arteries, and nerves. You can see the tissues and into the cells. You can also see the energy field around the body, the colors of the aura, and where there may be shadows or less light around you."

As the person shares with you what is seen, take note and redirect the focus back into the organs or areas that were darkened or shadowed. These will usually be the areas of physical imbalance or where mental patterns are creating blockages that could manifest into bodily dis-ease.

During crystal healings it is valuable to have paper and pen in hand to write down key words, phrases, or inspirations to read back to the recipient at appropriate moments during the therapy or to use afterwards in creating personal affirmations. Reading back specific words or phrases will trigger the reality of the experience and facilitate further recognition of the healing.

BUBBLE PROTECTION

As you refocus your client's attention into the darkened areas to see exactly what is in there creating the shadows, it is beneficial for the recipient to feel surrounded and protected with light. This creates more objectivity into whatever memories, thoughts or feelings are stored within the body and the auric field. The thoughts and feelings that will surface are the cause for the imbalance at hand. To imagine oneself surrounded in a bubble of impenetrable white light before viewing the situation more closely allows for a sense of protection and personal neutrality. Direct as follows:

> *"See yourself surrounded in a bubble of impenetrable light that allows you to clearly see exactly what is creating any area of darkness. Know that whatever you witness or recall, you are protected and within this bubble of light which separates you from the experience and allows you to view it with neutral perspective. Now let's observe and witness."*

Surrounding oneself in this manner allows personal identification to be with the light rather than with pain, disease, subconscious memories or darkness. Throughout the healing remind your client that protection is secured as deeper insight into the root causes of dis-ease are discovered. This bubble protection enables the recipient to be detached as traumatic subconscious memories are uncovered. It also creates a conscious connection with the light as a source of personal power and healing energy.

A woman came for a crystal healing whose hand was very tender and sore for no apparent reason. Azurite was laid on her third eye point to penetrate through the subconscious and Amethyst was placed above it to connect her with her intuition. Green Tourmaline was used at her shoulder, elbow and wrist to increase nerve conduction into her hand. Stones were placed on each of the chakra centers with an emphasis on the heart and solar plexus.

During the crystal healing we did the body overview in which she could not even see her hand from the elbow down; it appeared as a thick grey murky substance. After surrounding herself in a bubble of light she entered the grey area and immediately remembered an experience six weeks earlier when her daughter was missing for several hours. She had been so worried and upset that when she found her daughter she struck her and reprimanded her harshly for not communicating where she was going. The guilt that she had carried from hitting her child had gone so deep into the arm that it was now rendering her useless and in a state of pain. We then surrounded the heart center with many Rose Quartz and Green Aventurine stones and visualized self forgiveness, self love, and self understanding traveling into her arm on the inhale while exhaling the feelings of guilt and remorse. When we did a second body overview she could see her arm, the hand, and the fingers. As she inhaled healing energy into her hand and exhaled anxiety, I worked with a Clear Quartz generator crystal into points at the knuckles, wrist, elbow, shoulder and neck. At the end of the healing her wrist was more mobile and less painful. Her personal maintenance program included continued work with Rose Quartz and Green Aventurine as she focused on self-love and self-forgiveness.

SETTING THE STAGE

Another way to gain perspective and see into personal problem areas is with the image of a movie screen. Have your client imagine a gigantic stage in which old memories and suppressed feelings are going to be reenacted.

The Therapy

The actor or actress upon the stage will play out scenes from the past as they really occurred. The important aspect here is that the recipient remain in the audience watching and viewing the whole thing as a movie or a play that will unwind from the subconscious mind. Instead of associating with the actress or the actor, identification is made with the producer and the director; the person in charge that at any time can say "cut" and the scene will stop. This gives personal power to rework the past to the heart's desire.

This technique is best to use when one is getting in touch with painful childhood memories. It provides a way to see exactly what was felt and experienced in the past and empowers the conscious adult to go back into stressful situations to heal, soothe, and comfort.

I gave a lecture at Rircon College in Los Angeles and demonstrated a Basic Energy Charge Layout (see *Crystal Enlightenment, Vol. I*, page 38) on the director. When the quartz cluster was placed at the third eye he immediately recalled a traumatic experience that occurred when he was five years old. We incorporated the movie screen technique and his subconscious memory unfolded on the screen. When he was five years old, he had fallen on a piece of glass and had severely cut the side of his forehead and injured his eye. He was rushed to the emergency room of a hospital and was left alone, bleeding, on a table. His mother and the nurse were throwing up in one room next to him, while in another room he could overhear the doctors discuss whether he would be blind in that eye for the rest of his life. As it turned out, the glass was removed and his vision restored, but the trauma and feeling of abandonment that he had felt at that time was still being carried in his aura (over the side of his head where the injury occurred). What is also interesting is that when

I previously passed out crystals for the class to hold and experience, he instinctively was drawn to put the crystal up to that part of his head.

I then had him speak out loud and tell that scared little boy what he needed to hear. As his conscious adult self traversed the illusion of time, he went back and spoke words of comfort and reassured the traumatized child that he was not alone, and that everything turned out okay. In his mind he saw his adult self heal his child. He was able to release the trauma that had long since been forgotten, yet contributed to his present day feelings of abandonment and fear.

The movie screen technique is also one that can be used in personal meditation if the individual can stay identified with being the observer and the conscious adult in the present time. The crystal healer is responsible to help the recipient keep the identification as the director-producer and to guide the adult self back to embrace, comfort and heal the injured child.

TAKING CARE OF THE CHILD

The benefits of going back in the past to see where we have derived our attitudes and beliefs about life and where healing needs to be done is essential. It empowers us with the reassurance that we can nourish ourselves when other people couldn't or wouldn't. This is the foundation for forgiveness and provides the opportunity to accept full responsibility for ourselves instead of blaming life, people, or God for our pain. When the child-self within is healed and integrated with the conscious adult-self, emotional and mental patterns can change that have

The Therapy

evolved out of our often forgotten troubled past. It is then possible to come to terms with life, claim our power, and move our attention into what we choose our lives to be instead of being subconsciously manipulated by our own hurt child.

The child within us is that little girl or little boy that might have felt unloved, uncared for, or misunderstood at some point in life. It is also the innocence, the trust, and the belief in the magic of life. The child is sensitive and excited with each moment, exuding enthusiasm and joy that only unconditioned minds contain. It is a part of us that needs to be acknowledged and oftentimes healed. It is worth going back.

Rose Quartz and Green Aventurine are two of the best stones to use at the heart center when taking care of the child. Rose Quartz has the power to draw the energy of the heart inward, to heal the self, to change the self image through initiating self love. Rose Quartz will relay that forgiveness is the only way to gain inner peace as it teaches the importance of true caring. Rose Quartz understands, as no other stone can, that only compassion can fill in the gaps that external influences never could. With the wisdom of the heart activated through the use of the stone, it is possible to find within the self the true source of love and build a personal foundation of security that nothing can shake. Rose Quartz is the main heart center stone and is usually used in every crystal healing. Depending upon the person and the circumstances being worked with, Rose Quartz can safely be used in quantity.

Green Aventurine is also quartz (previewed on page 189) and is one of the most efficient healers around, lending its pure green ray into mental, emotional and physical realms. Used at the heart center, it will trigger the healing of the emotional body as well as any correlated physical dis-ease. Green Aventurine is like a good doctor that inspires you to get well, no matter what the problem is. Used in conjunction with Rose Quartz, a dynamic duo is formed that will focus on loving and healing the depths of the heart.

Use your intuition and creativity as you place these stones freely at the heart center. Use as much Rose Quartz and Green Aventurine as you feel is necessary in each healing. With these stones you need not worry about using too many or using them too often, as very little damage can occur from receiving too much love. It is important, however, to cleanse these stones after each use (see *Crystal Enlightenment, Vol. I,* for cleansing techniques).

EMOTIONAL RELEASE

When the recipient is getting in touch with past memories or feelings often there will be an intense emotional release. Have a box of tissues ready. Always allow these releases to occur. The expression and letting go of suppressed emotion is a key factor in the healing process. The role of the crystal healer is to facilitate the centering and refocusing of the identity back to the center line, back into the visualizations on the breath. This enables the emotional charge to neutralize in the conscious identification of the light and the center line. Often during emotional release, scenes with feelings attached may surface that have not been remembered since they occurred, yet are major factors in present day attitudes and conceptions about life. As the charge is released from suppressed feelings it is then possible to recreate the scene and give to oneself what is needed.

One woman that I worked with had a fear of intimacy and a deep feeling of abandonment. An Azurite nodule was placed at her third eye to penetrate through the fear of being close. Gem Silica stones were laid above and below the Azurite to open up greater insight into the matter. Several pieces of Rose Quartz surrounded a gem quality Kunzite at the heart center to focus the power of self-love into old memories and feelings. Malachite and Rhodochrosite resided at the solar plexus to surface root emotions and bridge the heart center to the navel. Citrine at the navel and Black Tourmaline on the groin points enabled self-nurturing to be integrated into her physical sense of well being.

When the stones were in place I initiated the movie screen technique and she traveled back to the time when she was four years old and broke her leg. She realized that she created that situation to try to get more love and nurturing from her parents. Instead of receiving the affection she had longed for, she was put in traction in a hospital while her parents went on a two week vacation. She was shedding tears when the nurse came in and remarked that she was not allowed to cry because it would upset the other children in the room. At that point in her childhood she closed off. During the crystal healing she gave herself permission to cry and released the suppressed emotions. This provided her with an opportunity to let go of years of bottled up feelings. Her cry was long and deep. When she was finished we then traveled back to that child while her conscious adult embraced, comforted, nourished and communicated love to her.

At times it is beneficial to place one hand over the heart center with the other on top of the head or at the navel to create a polarity in which emotional energy can recirculate itself. It is very important at these crucial times that you let the recipient know, as well as the child self that is being healed, that you are there for them, you love them, and you are sending that love and healing energy into the scene and into the heart of the matter. It is also advantageous to have the adult-self speak out loud to the child while you write it down. This can then become an affirmation that the client can use afterwards to reaffirm the healing that has occurred and integrate the well being of the child into their daily adult life.

THE SOLAR PLEXUS PURGERS

The release of suppressed emotion is facilitated by the use of several stones placed at the solar plexus. Malachite is the most powerful emotional purger and will, without a doubt, penetrate into unresolved emotions that have made their home at the solar plexus and blocked the gate-way into the heart. Malachite is to the emotional body what Azurite is to the mind; they both penetrate and bring into knowing that which lies beneath the surface, is unseen, and potentially dangerous.

Malachite also joins in partnership with Azurite (indigo) and Chrysocolla (sky, lake blue) to create unique entities unto themselves. The depths that Malachite-Azurite can reach together are unsurpassed by the power of the stones when used individually. Malachite-Azurite, when placed on either side of a large bulls-eye Malachite stone at the solar plexus, will trigger the mental correlations and subconscious memories associated with emotional stress. When Malachite-Chrysocolla is used to decorate a large Malachite at the solar plexus, the peaceful blue of Chrysocolla softens the indiscriminate purging of Malachite. Malachite-Chrysocolla stones can also be used alone on the solar plexus to ease the cleansing process and are often used when the effects of Malachite would be too severe or when a person is not ready to dive into the solar plexus pit. When Malachite joins with Chrysocolla and moves into the blue ray it is endowed with greater healing qualities and the ability to dissolve the emotional charge where Malachite alone cannot.

Malachite is one of the main stones that make the difference between a simple crystal healing layout that will basically balance energies and an advanced layout that is designed to clear that which is impeding spiritual growth. Malachite means "emotional release" and draws out, surfaces and reflects suppressed emotions. But alone Malachite does not have the crystalline power to dissolve them. It is therefore best to use Malachite with small single or double terminated Clear Quartz crystals placed around it. At least four crystals should point towards a large Malachite piece at the solar plexus to protect the Malachite from absorbing too much emotional energy from the recipient as well as assisting the client in discharging the surfacing emotions.

Rhodochrosite is also a very effective stone to use above or below Malachite in crystal healing layouts to assimilate and digest emotional upheaval. Bearing a true peach color, Rhodochrosite successfully blends the orange-yellow of the navel with the pink of the heart, and in so doing establishes a harmonious relationship between both energy centers. Rhodochrosite alone at the solar plexus will bridge and harmonize the lower centers with the upper ones and create a sense of integration between the physical and spiritual bodies.

All of the above stones are explained in *Crystal Enlightenment, Vol. I.* Knowledge of their specific energies and effects combined with the therapeutic techniques given herein will enable positive emotional release to occur and open the channels of love to flow into the heart center.

CHAPTER IV
TIME BRIDGING

We have been conditioned and programmed to view time as a linear event with a beginning, a duration, and an end. Being born in the conception of this reality, we also see ourselves as being linear and the reality of life as being third dimensional. Even those who are aware that they have lived before and have had other existences at other times and places still often see that as past and life now as present with the future ahead, in the distance.

The life that we are living now is but one facet of who we are. Potentially we are multi-dimensional beings that have the power to advance our state of consciousness (as a race) into the fourth dimension—the fourth chakra, the heart, and embody the power of love. Our essence as a being will never cease to exist. It will change form a myriad of times and express itself in a multitude of ways. We will dance on this earth and then on into the stars and into the light at the center of the galaxy. In order to do this we need to change our concepts about life and death, about time, about ourselves and the universe of which we are a part. Healing ourselves of the wounds that plague our hearts and limit the expression of love is the first step.

During crystal healings the illusion of time can be dissolved and the reality of the eternal moment experienced. When viewing life out of linear sequence it is possible to identify with the essence of the Self that lives each lifetime and discover the culmination of all life experience. Then all of our past lives, the life that we are aware of now, and the ones that are happening in the future can all merge into a present state of conscious awareness. When the totality of being unites with the eternal moment of cosmic time, the ultimate reality is experienced and assimilated.

In that state of awareness it is possible to bridge the span of time between lives, whether past or future, and to unite the simultaneous expressions of personality, ego and purpose into one united being—one oversoul who is in tune with the eternal presence of the "Now." As we learn to time travel in this way, it will be possible to integrate the lessons of each life experience and create a bridge that will link our parallel existences and fragmented aspects of identity into one unified sense of self. Imagine the freedom of creating peace and joy within the third dimension yet not being bound by time or space!

Lifetimes may have passed since the soul had conscious communication with the light. For some, generations and millenium have gone by without the personal direction and guidance from inner resources. Now, with advanced crystal healing techniques designed for past and future life therapy, it is possible to once again receive the blessings from the spiritual realms within the Self and accelerate personal evolution.

PAST–FUTURE LIFE THERAPY

There seems to be a lot of emotional sensationalism surrounding past life recall, and it is exciting when one has the knowledge and experience of living before. But the purpose of remembering such identities is not to build an ego image around it, but rather to learn the lessons that are involved in past or future existences that often have karmic repercussions in this life. Ideally, it is far superior to have one's identity fixed within the eternal moment in which rests all power, all knowing, all presence, and all peace.

When crystals are used in the aura and Amethyst, Gem Silica, Azurite and Luvulite stones are placed on the third eye center, the mind can be, at least temporarily, cleansed of the illusions and narrow concepts that can consume the consciousness. In this state it is possible to see through and beyond the limitations inherent in the tunnel vision of linear thinking. Time and reality as we have come to know it will be shattered upon experiencing the unlimited dimensions that exist in the full scope of third eye vision. Imagine seeing our small planet Earth from the viewpoint of the sun or expanding the perspective even wider to witness our Milky Way Galaxy from the center of the cosmos. This type of consciousness can be initiated when the mind is free from the third dimensional reality and expands into the infinity of spirit.

The purpose of past life regression or future life progression is to clear whatever magnets exist in our past or future expressions that keep our consciousness and actions attached to the illusion of time and space. We presently use only about one-tenth of our brain capacity. We are capable of expanding our thoughts to encompass the entire expanse of the universe. When we live as fragmented beings with part of our identity bound to the past or the future, it is impossible to utilize the mind to its fullest extent. The potential of past-future life therapy is to untie the knots in our multi-existing selves and create a bridge of consciousness between them upon which the light of the soul can traverse.

In crystal healings past-future life recall does not occur unless the present life is being affected by something specific in another existence that needs to be cleared up and learned from in order to gain knowledge or complete a cycle in this lifetime. When a person has been born with a hereditary or congenital dis-ease or when drastic circumstances occur within the first three to five years of life, it indicates that karma from another life is involved. In these circumstances the effects of a past or future existence come into immediate play in the present lifetime.

Just as the adult self bridges time and goes back to care for the child, the past or future lifetime is going to be paid a visit by its alter-self, which is you now. In this unique opportunity you can actually serve as a guide or a guardian angel to an aspect of your self that is simultaneously existing in a parallel reality within a different time zone. With the help of the light force generated by crystal power, it is possible to actually change past history, to recreate it by learning the lessons now from the events in the past. To consciously rewrite a bygone time and rework it to our positive purpose can have immeasurable positive effects on the life we are living now. In the same way, be open and receptive to receiving communication from your future-self who may be offering guidance and direction to you now.

ADVANCED CRYSTAL HEALING LAYOUTS

Any of the Third Eye Awakeners (see page 54) can be used at the brow during crystal healing layouts to initiate alter life recall. The most powerful stones in this category are gem quality Azurite nodules or wands and high grade Luvulite. The power these stones possess when used together can penetrate the depth of the subconscious mind where all experience has been recorded (Azurite) and bring that into concrete knowledge relevant to present day circumstances (Luvulite). With an Azurite nodule on the third eye center and a piece of Luvulite placed above it, personal akashic records can be accessed.

Another powerful combination to use at the third eye center is Gem Silica with a clear double terminated Quartz crystal placed above it, one termination pointing towards the stone with the other directed at the crown chakra. A second double terminated Quartz crystal can be placed at the top of the head with one termination directed towards the crown chakra and the other extending into the aura. The Gem Silica will expand the inner vision to witness simultaneous existences as the double terminated crystals make the necessary connections.

It is important when applying either of these layouts that stones are also placed upon the navel center, groin points and feet to balance the expansion of the head centers. Tiger's Eye is the best stone to place at the navel to ground and integrate the golden energies of the crown with the physical realities. Dark green-black Tourmaline at the groin will channel the higher frequencies into the body to be assimilated for physical healing and well being.

(Continued on page 66)

CRYSTAL
AND
STONE LAYOUTS

THE THIRD EYE AWAKENERS

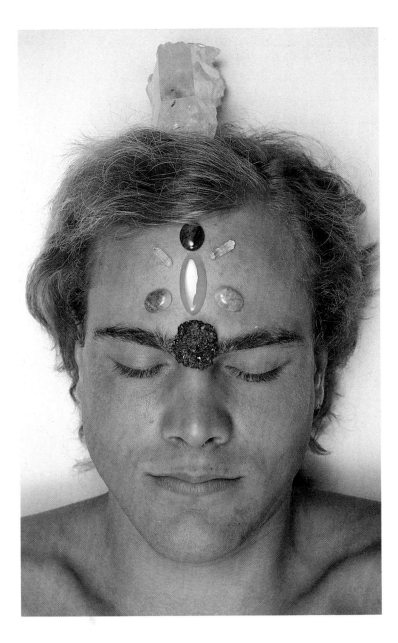

THE COMMUNICATORS

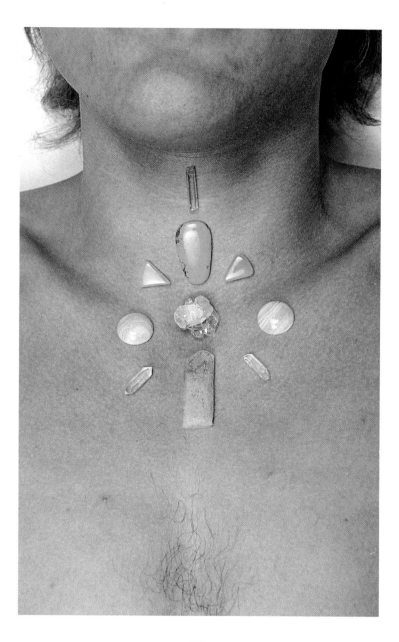

THE HEART HEALERS

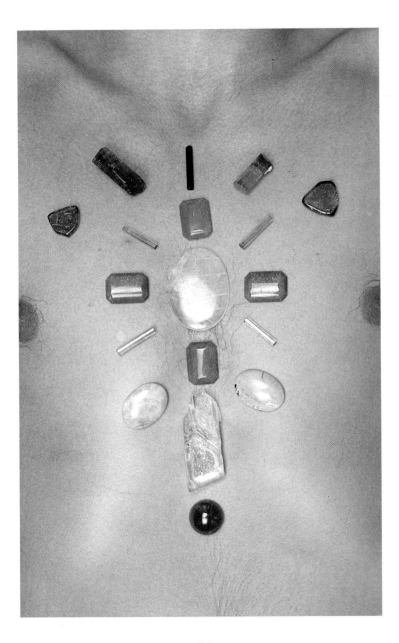

THE SOLAR PLEXUS PURGERS

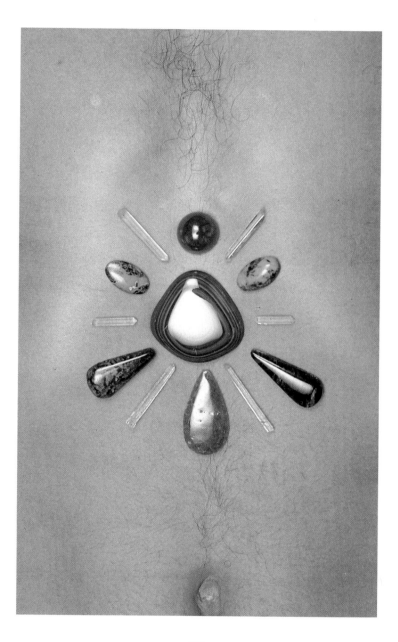

THE NAVEL CONNECTION

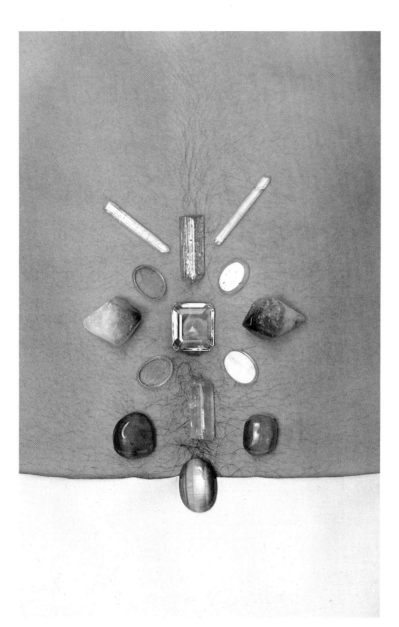

THE ENERGIZING AND GROUNDING STONES

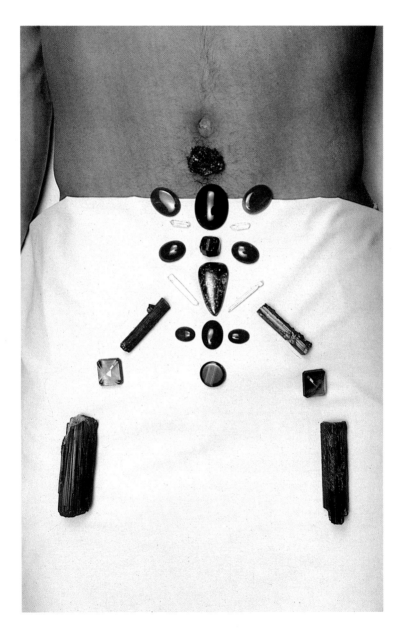

THE FULL BODY LAYOUT

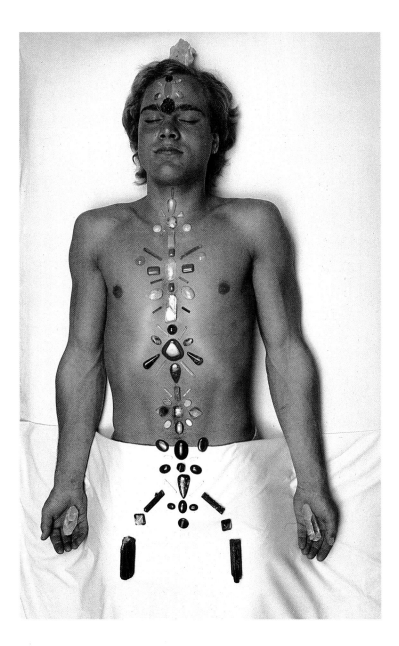

A CRYSTAL HEALING WITH KATRINA

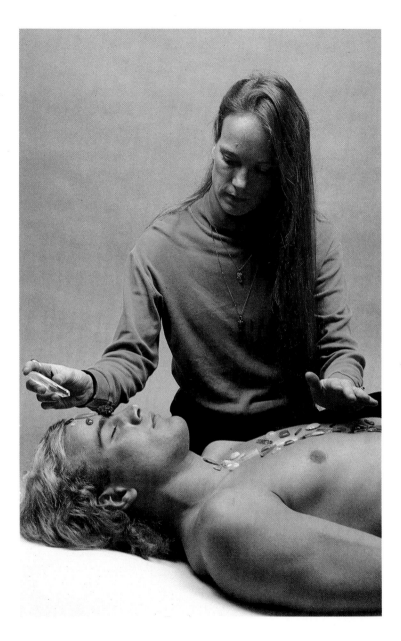

THE THIRD EYE AWAKENERS

Between the eyebrows rests an Azurite nodule to pene-trate through subconscious blockages. Directly above it resides a beautiful Gem Silica stone to expand the vision into the realm of spirit. On either side of the Silica rests two Amethyst cabs to initiate a meditative experience. At the hairline Lord Luvulite rules who relays understanding into the higher mind. It is connected to the Gem Silica through two double terminated Clear Quartz crystals below it. To usher in white light into the crown chakra a large Clear Quartz generator crystal has been placed with the termination touching the crown point.

THE COMMUNICATORS

Directly on the throat chakra point has been placed a gem quality Celestite crystal cluster to facilitate the expression of the highest truth. Below it is a naturally terminated Aquamarine crystal, channeling energy from the heart with the help of two double terminated Clear Quartz crys-tals on each side. To ground the effects Blue Lace Agate rests on either side of the Celestite with Turquoise directly above it. Charging the Turquoise is Gem Silica on both sides and a gem quality Indicolite above, ushering energy in from the third eye.

THE HEART HEALERS

In the center of the chest is the heart's corner stone, Rose Quartz, initiating self-love and compassion. It has been surrounded on four sides by the healing energy of the Green Aventurine with small Pink Tourmaline wands placed inbetween them for the expansion of love. Five Pink and Green Tourmaline pieces cover the upper chest to facilitate the heart's expression into words at the throat center. Kunzite rests below the bottom Green Aventurine to activate the heart chakra and is accompanied on either side by the grounding energies of Rhodonite. A gem quality Rhodochrosite has been placed at the solar plexus point to bridge the loving energy of the heart into the navel center.

THE SOLAR PLEXUS PURGERS

In the center of the solar plexus resides a large bullseye Malachite to penetrate through suppressed emotion. It has been surrounded by six Clear Quartz generators to dissolve whatever is mirrored and surfaced. On the upper right and left sides of the Malachite rests Malachite-Chrysocholla while below Malachite-Azurite stones have been placed on the lower right and left sides. With gem quality Rhodochrosite above and below the Malachite, the way is cleared for energy to flow between the heart center and the navel chakra.

THE NAVEL CONNECTION

On the navel point is a gem quality faceted Citrine which is being charged by two naturally terminated Citrine generators on each side. Naturally terminated golden Topaz crystals are also pointing towards the faceted Citrine as well as four small Rutilated Quartz cabs at each corner to further energize the chakra. Two Clear Quartz generators are activating the upper Topaz. With Amber to either side of the lower Topaz and Tigereye as the base stone the higher frequencies of the golden ray are grounded into the body.

THE ENERGIZING AND GROUNDING STONES

Below the navel resides a true red Realgar cluster with a deep red Carnelian cabachon directly below it to stimulate the creative energy of the second (sexual) chakra. To either side are smaller, more orange Carnelian cabs. Small double terminated Quartz crystals accentuate the power of these stones. Beneath the middle Carnelian is a natural Garnet crystal accompanied on each side by Red Jasper to ground the creative energies. A Realgar cabachon sums up the red stones and is charged by two Clear Quartz generators on each side. Receiving the red energies into the first center are three red-flecked Bloodstones (center stone larger, sided by two smaller). Hawkeye is directly below grounding healing energies directly into the body. To activate the base chakra gem quality Smoky Quartz rests on each groin point. Large dark green Tourmaline wands are found above and below the faceted stones to channel energy into the body to strengthen the physical systems.

THE FULL BODY LAYOUT

The full body layout is a combination of the previous individual layouts described. Clear Quartz crystals were also placed in the hands and at the feet with the terminations pointing in, towards the body, to circulate healing energy.

Naturally terminated Smoky Quartz crystals pointing in at the feet will complete the circulation of energy.

When working with layouts with the intention of bridging time into altered lives, it is necessary to have at least one stone on each of the chakra points to center and balance the entire chakra system while moving the consciousness into other dimensions. The higher octave throat stones are best to use at the throat center to channel through the voice what is seen and experienced in alter states. These stones would be: Aquamarine, Celestite, and Gem Silica.

A Clear Quartz generator can be used in the aura after the initial stone placement and held for fifteen seconds above each main chakra stone (beginning at the base) to charge each one of the centers and balance the subtle energy systems. When the generator reaches the third eye and crown points, be sensitive and intuitive to responses that will serve to guide the crystal's further movement. Perhaps you will feel that the crystal is directing you to rotate in a clockwise direction to open the third eye, or you might sense that to actually touch the third eye stone would be of benefit. There is no set rule, it depends on the circumstances, the person, and the moment.

INITIATING PAST-FUTURE LIFE RECALL

At times during the course of crystal healings images will appear that have no apparent meaning or memory attached to them. These impressions may occur when looking into the shadow areas of the aura in a body overview

66

or often result as feelings are traced back to their source. Whenever they occur, acknowledge them and broaden the scope by looking deeper into it and allowing the subconscious memory tapes to play. Again, during these times use the bubble protection and keep yourself identifying with the light traveling through the center line with each breath. Any emotional charge can be neutralized and the effects of karmic ties be learned from and released if the consciousness remains fixed on the light, on the higher self. Otherwise, it is very easy to get overinvolved with past life identities and miss the overall picture. The role of the crystal healer in this type of therapy is to keep guiding the consciousness of the recipient back into the light to view the scene from the center line perspective. The job of the person being healed is to be willing to let go, to release, and surrender it all into the light at the source of their being. This very willingness is what allows for the acknowledgment of personal lessons, the decharging of suppressed emotion, the healing of the body, and the self actualization of the soul.

I was working with a woman who felt she was very heavy in the thighs, which was affecting her self-image and her ability to attract a meaningful relationship into her life. She felt very disassociated and uncomfortable with her body from the hips down. A high quality Luvulite was partnered with Gem Silica and Azurite at the third eye to penetrate the subconscious and gain higher vision and understanding. Gem Silica was also used at the throat to facilitate verbal expression of what the inner sight witnessed. Rose Quartz and Pink Tourmaline formed a beautiful mandala of love at the heart to be used for self-healing and expression. A naturally terminated Citrine crystal at the navel was pointing towards three pieces of high grade Carnelian placed in a triangular fashion on the second chakra to direct her personal power and creative energy into her legs and thighs. Dark green and black Tourmaline crystals were placed at the instep of each foot, on the ankles, knees, hips and groin points with the terminations pointing down to direct and ground energy into the lower part of her body. With Malachite at the solar plexus to mirror suppressed emotions and Rhodochrosite below it to bridge the heart to the navel we were ready to proceed into therapeutics.

Initiating the body overview she saw dark clouds around her thighs, particularly the right one. Surrounding her in light with the bubble protection, we entered the darkened area and she immediately started seeing images of herself as a man in the early 1900's in the thick forests of Canada. She (he) was chopping wood by his log cabin for the winter and accidentally cut his thigh when the ax slipped out of his hand. Being so far away from the town, he was unable to get proper medical care and as a result had to have his right leg amputated, leaving his wife and small child without a "man" around the house. He was unable to work and felt more useless and irritable as the years went by. He had incredible guilt and felt as if he had failed as a husband and a father. (This would affect her ability to attract a meaningful relationship into her life now.) At this time I used a Clear Quartz generator crystal and directed healing energy into points on her toes, ankles, knees, thighs and hips, especially the right one.

In traversing time, my client bridged her consciousness to his and guided him to make the best of the situation and not to indulge in his own self pity, but instead to do whatever was in front of him and to embrace all that came into his life. As the subconscious of the man received the message, she planted seeds that would affect the rest of his life in a positive way. She then rewrote her memory; instead of the man dying feeling worthless, she saw him learn from his experience as he began to appreciate life for what it was. As a result of this, he was able to go beyond his limitations and become stronger because of it. After the crystal healing my client felt as if she, herself, was incorporating the lessons that he had learned. Her legs felt open and free and she felt more stable on the earth. She was aware that she had rewritten her personal history and as a result each simultaneous life was bettered by it.

As you are working with a person and the memory begins to unwind, allow for the complete verbal expression of what is being experienced so that you can assist in the understanding of how those events tie into present circumstances and what the overall lesson is to be learned. Oftentimes the crystal healer will have insights and a broader perspective of the implications as it is possible to be more neutral when it is not your personal experience.

TRACING

One of the techniques that is used in past life recall is called tracing. Here, we single out a feeling that has been prevalent throughout a person's life, say anger, fear or sorrow. There will be many times in the course of this life when basic situations will have repeated themselves and played out the drama of the emotion. When tracing, guide the person back through the present life to the major memories involving the feeling. As you do this, decharge each memory with the breath and take care of the past selves in this life—the teenager, the adolescent, the child, and the infant. Often this process alone can take several crystal healing sessions before enough clearing has been done to allow the conscious mind to bridge itself into a past or future life. As you work your way back to the initial memory in this life, be prepared for images or subtle impressions to surface from the deeper levels of the subconscious. Direct your client to stay relaxed and breathe through the center line as you instruct:

"Become very still, open, and receptive to the memory or feeling of other expressions of yourself in a different time frame. Immediately acknowledge without a doubt any impression that will enter your mind and allow that memory to unwind as the scene unfolds before you."

(Here you may also want to incorporate the movie screen and bubble protection technique.)

As the recollection of events is acknowledged, it is important to keep a very conscious connection to the soul level through the breath and the center line focus. As the images are decharged and it becomes evident what the lessons involved are, it is also important to come to the understanding of just why it was necessary to attract all of the circumstances and what the culmination of the entire experience is. It is possible at this time to call upon inner wisdom to give to the conscious mind the specific purpose behind all parallel events. With this comprehension it is feasible to neutralize the karmic patterns, cleanse and seal the aura, reap the harvest of lifetimes of experience, and align with a personal source of light and energy to be consciously manifested from that point on.

TIME REVERSAL

Another method of initiating past life recall is by having your client visualize a clock in front of them. As they watch it, the clock begins to go in a counterclockwise direction as the images of their life are superimposed over the clock. Gradually guide them back to the memories of yesterday, of last week, of last year. All the time the hands on the clock are spinning faster and faster. (This technique can also be used over several crystal healing sessions in conjunction with the tracing procedure to work out and clear charged memories and feelings locked back in time in this present life.) As the clock spins backward in time to birth, pre-birth, conception and past life, ask the soul's presence to guide the mind to the time of relevant significance in relation to whatever is being worked on. Most often images will immediately flood the mind and scenes from past lives enter the inner vision. Here, it is again important to take the conscious adult-self of the present back to comfort, guide and balance the alter-self existing in the past. This is where the actual bridging of consciousness occurs and the illusion of time is penetrated.

I worked with a woman who was kidnapped and raped when she was four years old. She was unable to trust in God because she was not protected and this horrible event was allowed to occur. She was also presently recovering from a hysterectomy which we had already determined was a result of the trauma of this experience.

Surrounding a Gem Silica with eight small double terminated Clear Quartz crystals at the third eye, and pointing a large double terminated tabular Quartz at the crown, the connections were made to enable her mind to

71

enter into an alternate time zone. Aquamarine at the throat allowed verbal expression of altered vision and Carnelian at the second chakra sparked creative energy. Six Green Tourmaline pieces were placed at the heart center to strengthen her against the painful memories of her youth and a naturally terminated Topaz crystal pointed towards a rutilated Quartz at the navel to empower her will. Malachite and Rhodochrosite cleared and opened the solar plexus as faceted Smoky Quartz on the groin points and Black Tourmaline at the feet facilitated to ground her crystal healing experience into reality.

Initiating the time reversal method, she was taken back in her genetic memory to when she had been in a position of power in Russia and had used her sexual energy to manipulate and control leaders at that time to serve her own selfish purpose. Coming to this realization, she understood why she had been raped at a young age and was defenseless in the situation. She forgave herself for her abuse of sexual power in her past life and nurtured the injured child in her present life. After integrating the cumulative lessons she then felt capable of consciously using her personal creative energies for positive purposes.

The image of the clock can also be used to initiate future life progression by visualizing the hands moving forward in a clockwise direction.

PRE-BIRTH PURPOSE

Using the techniques mentioned above, it is of benefit, in some circumstances, to remain in the interim period between conception and life to view the decisions that were being made then by the soul as to when and where it needed to be born to have the proper cultures and surroundings to learn specific lessons. From the pre-birth perspective it is possible to see the purpose for choosing specific parents and to see what patterns were chosen to unfold throughout the life course and what lessons were the objective. This time zone is one where the soul's knowledge can most easily be contacted because it is not attached to a specific physical form. This is the time when decisions are made and life's course is mapped out. Tapping into this neutral space is of great benefit in coming to understand why you, personally, are responsible for attracting all of your circumstances. Attuning to this state of awareness allows you to see what choices were made that dictated life's events for personal growth and evolution. Then the reason behind bewildering circumstances becomes clear and alignment with this understanding makes it possible to actively initiate conscious action in the choices made henceforth.

When working with the Pre-Birth Purpose technique it is important that the knowledge of the pre-life decisions come from the inner guidance of your client and not from you, the healer. (The role of the healer is to assist the client to access the source of their own knowledge.) Tapping into personal resources is very important for the recipients of crystal healings, as it enables them to know exactly why their life has unfolded the way it has. With this understanding, based on their personal experience with themselves, it is much easier to accept full responsibility for the healing process.

SCANNING

This is an advanced procedure that is used only when the recipient has the mental discipline necessary to completely detach and disassociate from any identification attached to the present life. This free floating capacity of mind provides the impetus for altered vision which oftentimes initiates past or future life recall. It is possible to even will it to occur if the recipient has developed adequate mental power. Again, the purpose for doing this is to break a mental pattern or habit that is affecting this lifetime. For example, if a person knows that they had a past life in Egypt that has a direct effect on life now, one could choose to align their consciousness with that time frequency and recall specific circumstances to observe and learn from. By scanning ancient or future memory tapes for the exact time sequence, past or future life recall is accomplished and conscious communication with alter egos can be made. These alter selves may also be researching their future or past selves, which could be you now. This type of experience is one that changes the quality of life forever because you come to know yourself as a part of a much larger Self and your consciousness can merge with that "over-soul" and align with the source of all being. This personally empowering experience can be initiated by those who have developed their minds to the degree of being able to consciously disassociate from the present lifetime.

CHAPTER V
THE HEALING

EXORCISING—RELEASING
NEGATIVE ENERGIES

Exorcism, as defined in this book, is the ability to assist one to free oneself from negative influences or entities. The crystals (particularly Clear Quartz) play an important role in strengthening the forces of light in order to accomplish this. You may never attract anyone who needs to be exorcised. But if you pursue an active crystal healing practice, the chances are that you will. The following information is based on my experience with these encounters in my crystal healing practice over the last eight years. I encourage you to use it if the need arises and suggest that you further research the subject if you choose to concentrate in this area.

The nature of demons is twofold. Often we are possessed by our own negative habit patterns that gain control over our conscious functioning. These habitual tendencies can, in and of themselves, become as living entities within us that usurp our personal power and render us incapable of functioning in accordance with our own higher will. Such emotional barriers can often make us act as if we are under the possession of an alien force, and it is foreign to the true nature of our being. In this type of circumstance it is possible, through the development of will and the activation of the light force through crystals to overcome our own demons of anger, jealousy, fear, greed, sorrow, etc., that can bind one to continual pain and lack of personal control. In crystal healings it is possible to bring in enough light to dissolve the fiendish spirits that are born out of insecurity with the self.

The other type of demon frequently encountered is actually an outside entity that has attached itself to the auric body of a person and feeds on their vital force. These demonic influences can manipulate the subconscious to behave in certain manners. This type of possession usually occurs when a person is also plagued to a large degree by personal emotional demons resulting in a weak and vulnerable auric field. In these cases as well, bringing more light and energy into the aura through crystal healings will serve to exorcise the forces of darkness and ignorance by evoking the inner light to strengthen personal resources.

The most important factor in this type of advanced crystal healing practice is to claim complete authority over the forces at hand and demand and command that they either come into alignment and integrate themselves with the individual's purpose or they must leave, never to return. On occasion the demonic presence will choose to alter itself and integrate with the soul's higher characteristics. Most of the time, however, they choose to move on as they are unable to align with the light. As they leave, send them off with love and an affirmation that they will eventually come to serve the light. Then release them forever from the consciousness.

In either type of case, working with negative influences is an opportunity to gain individual control over the forces and tendencies that can invade the human character. Whether the demons are personal attitudes and uncontrolled emotional responses or external entities, the key to dismissal is to be fearless and claim conscious authority over them. Often when dealing with demons in crystal healings the person possessed will have given up the right to exorcise personal control over them. This subconscious surrender is what feeds these foreign parasites and sucks the life-light force out of an individual, rendering them helpless against themselves.

Crystal healing is a very effective way to eliminate the demonic forces that plague human character and integrity. It is very important for the crystal healer to be courageous in these situations and to direct the recipient to be the same. As the crystal healing reveals the fiendish personal neurotic patterns or the external entity that has attached itself to the aura, keep a sense of humor and direct your client to focus on their center line and identify with the internal source of light. Claim absolute command and offer a choice of surrender and integration, or dismissal. Usually there will be vivid visualization within the mind of the receiver of the demons that can be worked with as you (the healer) add input that will strengthen your client's new self-image.

When working with demonic influences the most effective crystal to use is Clear Quartz. Small clusters can be placed on each chakra point with double terminated Quartz Crystals in between each center to integrate the energy systems. Single Quartz Generator Crystals can be placed at the crown, in the hands and at the soles of the feet with the terminations pointing into the body to direct more light force into circulation. Clear Quartz with its dynamic charge and white light radiance, when used in quantity, is a stronger force than any prevailing darkness. It is important to properly cleanse these crystals (sun and water method) following such exorcisms.

I was working with a man who had an uncontrollable violent temper and as a result of it his family life was crumbling. On several occasions his anger had gotten so out of control that he had struck his wife and child. In a crystal healing he was embraced in Clear Quartz light as we traced the feeling back to the time when he was a child and had been beaten by his stepfather, whom his mother was with instead of his real father, whom he loved dearly. In his mind he saw his anger as an ugly red demon with sharp teeth that was eating away at his heart. I encouraged him to visualize a healing blue energy entering into his heart on the inhale (a calming antidote for the angry red) and to release the blistering red anger on the exhale. Blue and green stones were also placed at the heart center, i.e., Green Aventurine, Gem Silica, and Blue Lace Agate. We then traversed time and his conscious adult self comforted the little boy who was mad at his mother for leaving his father, angry at his father for leaving, and furious at his stepfather for being there and abusing him. He also released the anger at himself as he let go of his sense of personal responsibility for somehow being the cause of the whole thing. As we worked, the ugly red demon's power subsided and he saw that underneath was his vulnerable sensitive self, which he was then able to better integrate into his being and into his life.

The Healing

There have also been times during the course of crystal healing sessions when I have sensed demons of outside origin. In one case the demon actually started to psychically attack me as I worked with my client to gain power over it. In this case I grabbed my Black Obsidian ball (which I rarely use in crystal healings) and held it in front of me for protection against the dark force. (See *Crystal Enlightenment, Vol. I*, Black Obsidian page 93.) Affirming our power of light over the evil presence, we successfully dismissed it and my client achieved increased confidence and ability to control her own life.

On occasion, when releasing powerful negative energies, it may be necessary to place Black Obsidian stones at the third eye or heart center to gain clearer understanding as to the nature of the evil and its source. Black Obsidian will bluntly and relentlessly mirror the darkened areas of the mind in order to establish connection with the superconscious. Black Obsidian should only be used when both the healer and the receiver are aware of its effects and are prepared to process the inevitable changes that will occur. Even then the Obsidian stones should be surrounded by at least four double terminated Clear Quartz crystals to dissolve any elements of the fearful unknown as they arise (please refer to *Crystal Enlightenment, Vol. I*, pages 93–100).

To a large degree healing occurs when we are willing to clear the negative forces that are not serving our personal unfoldment. First, it is a matter of realizing that there are attitudes, emotions, or outside entities that must be released. Then an acknowledgment for the need of change, followed by the courage to look inside the darkened areas of oneself. Finally the fearless authority of the conscious will can dissolve any shadows blocking the inner light.

MIND, BODY, HEART,
SOUL CORRELATIONS

The body is the most dense form of matter that we possess. The soul is the most subtle, connecting to an infinite source of spiritual light and energy. The mental and emotional bodies exist in between the physical and spiritual bodies. When any aspect of the self is out of alignment with the light of the soul then imbalance occurs. The connection between the spiritual, mental, emotional and physical bodies is very real, yet unseen and often unacknowledged. During crystal healing practices it is possible to see the direct correlations between the different facets of the self and how one interacts and influences the rest. Often the mental patterns and attitudes will trigger emotional responses and the emotions will register somewhere in the body.

The physical plane is a manifestation of the more subtle realms. The health of our body is a reflection of our thoughts and feelings. The planetary wellness is the result of our collective thinking. As we gain conscious control over our thoughts and align the mind and body with the light at the source of our beings, we will have the ability to fulfill our greatest potential. The spirit will flow through each individual and manifest its creative intelligence in a myriad of unique and fascinating forms.

Physical illness is one of the last signs that reflects that the mental, emotional or material body is out of alignment with the light. The body is usually the final phase of manifestation, reflecting a disharmonious relationship with the self. Dis-ease is a biofeedback system that says "Take note, something's wrong here, better investigate." With proper insight the body can be easily read.

A woman with lupus, which is a dis-ease where the immune system becomes confused and starts attacking the red blood cells, traces past feelings of confusion with associated suicidal tendencies. A man who feels that he doesn't have a "leg to stand on" has chronically weak ankles and knees. A child who needs to wear glasses at age three obviously is having a hard time looking at and adjusting to life. Attitudes of close-mindedness and "I just don't want to hear about it" can create difficulties hearing. The psychological and emotional implications of physical dis-ease are always present and can be a main clue as to what healing needs to be done and on what level. Complete healing can only occur when the mental patterns, attitudes and feelings which are responsible for the physical imbalance are understood, learned from, and transformed.

When the mind is attuned to the spirit unforetold insight and wisdom can be gained. From that source springs the wellspring of creation. With proper mental alignment the very act of projecting a thought can create the reality. The thoughts of peace, health, joy, and love can create an aura of healing energy that others can benefit from by merely being in your presence. The creative possibilities are far-reaching as we learn to heal ourselves and let go of any belief or any limitation that is less than our true potential.

THE HEART HEALERS

There are several main heart center stones that can be used in an infinite number of combination and design on the chest during crystal healing layouts to heal with the power of love. In addition to the heart trinity of Rose Quartz, Kunzite and Pink Tourmaline, several other stones deserve recognition as major heart center healers. They are Rhodonite, Green Aventurine, Green Tourmaline, and Rhodochrosite.

Rose Quartz is the cornerstone for the heart's foundation exemplifying self-love, forgiveness, and inner peace. Kunzite will activate the power of love while Pink Tourmaline dynamically expresses it. (Each one of these stones are explained in depth in *Crystal Enlightenment, Vol. I.*)

Rhodonite solidifies the power of love into day to day action while Green Aventurine has the ability to soothe and heal whatever ails you. Green Tourmaline strengthens the emotional body in preparation for the highest expression of feeling and peachy Rhodochrosite will bridge the solar plexus to connect the navel power with the heart, harmoniously blending physical and spiritual energies.

When using any of these stones at the heart during crystal healing layouts, be aware of the specific purpose of each and use the stones in a manner that will create the desired effect. An advanced heart chakra layout for general overall purposes could be performed by placing a large Rose Quartz at the center of the chest to draw the energy within for personal renewal. Four Green Aventurine stones are placed in each direction around the Rose Quartz to bring in healing energy. Lay at least four pieces of Pink and/or Green Tourmaline on the upper chest directed towards the throat to channel the strength of love into the throat chakra for clear verbal expression. Rhodochrosite at the solar plexus with Kunzite directly above and Rhodonite below will activate the healing power of love and usher it into the navel to be put into direct use in daily activities.

In whatever manner or combination these heart healers are used, they bring the reality of compassion into personal experience. These stones become your best friends in a crystal healing practice as they beautifully relay various expressions and lessons of love.

RELEASING, CLEARING, LETTING GO

Our healing lies in the ability and the willingness to let go of whatever is inhibiting union with the Self. This process can often lead one into many drastic changes in life as old associations, relationships, careers, and habit patterns fall away. The letting go process can be one that pulls on many heart strings as the new self is propelled towards people of like-mindedness and environments where inner development can be nurtured. Sometimes people create serious dis-eases as a way to wake up and initiate radical change in their lives. Even though the sacrifice seems great, the rewards of living in tune with one's own higher consciousness cannot be surpassed by anything else that life can offer. It is often like you are being reborn and yet maintaining the same body.

This rebirth into spirit is the opportunity of transformation that each and every individual has before them at

every moment. Letting go of all the false securities and
ego associations will harvest into a wealth of health and
joy. This is only accomplished when courage and faith
plunge you into the black hole of your own fears, only to
willfully emerge into the light at the other side. Personal
dedication and commitment to this process are the cata-
lysts that enable an incredible acceleration of spiritual
growth to unfold in one's life. Crystals serve to dissolve
the shadows of falsehood that can shadow inner radiance
while strengthening and reinforcing the power of will and
self control.

Once this process has been initiated it may take
months or even years to be completely reborn, but each
day brings a little more clarity, a little more strength.
Each conscious breath brings you a little closer to the
source of your own being, each glance at a crystal reminds
you of the light, and the effects are cumulative. You will
grow, and as you do, personal transformation and empowerment are the natural results. The healing presence is
awaiting your continual recognition and access into your
daily affairs. It is there now. Healing is just a breath away.

CONCLUDING THE HEALING

In the natural flow of the crystal healing session there will
usually evolve a perfect time to end the healing. It is generally after a major shift has occurred or realization has
been made. It is best not to try to "do it all" in one session
as the recipient will need time to digest and assimilate the
experience and incorporate the effects through a personal
maintenance plan. Therefore, it is most advantageous to
conclude the healing at the time that will seem most

appropriate to the healer. Crystal healings, in my experience, take at least two hours from the time the client walks in the door until an adequate maintenance plan is worked out, and it is not something that can be rushed. The more crystal healings you do, the greater sense you will gain as to the most opportune time to wind up each session.

It is important to have the recipient breathe very deeply and completely before reopening the eyes to the physical world. Direct as follows:

"Breathe fully and completely (especially into the main areas where healing occurred) and bring your light and healing energy into your body. Feel it circulating in your blood stream and through your nervous system. Direct the light within your center line into every cell, every tissue and organ. Breathe it into your legs and through the soles of your feet. Now, I would like you to prepare to open your eyes. When you do I am going to hand you a mirror and the first image you will see will be of yourself and the stones that have been placed upon your body. This will be an affirmation and a physical manifestation of the healing that has occurred and of the beauty of your own inner light. Now, when you feel ready, slowly open your eyes."

Have a mirror ready and the moment your client opens the eyes gently touch the heart center and state, *"We affirm the light and the healing that has been done,"* then hand the recipient the mirror and allow your client to gaze at the beauty of light and color as it has been displayed on the body.

There is not a set rule for the removal of stones. Generally stones surrounding main chakra stones come off first, leaving the stones that were primary in the healing on until last. For example, if the healing revolves around the ability to clearly express one's thoughts and feelings, the throat chakra stones would be the last to come off. It is also most beneficial to leave the base chakra stones and those at the knees or feet on until the end to continue to ground the energies of the healing into the body. Wipe each stone off with a damp cotton cloth as you remove it and place the stones that will need extra cleansing aside to purify with the sun and water method (Malachite, Rose Quartz, etc.) The rest can go on a Quartz cluster or be smudged (see page 173).

After a healing the recipient will usually feel a little spaced out and disoriented. It is the responsibility of the crystal healer to make sure that your client is thoroughly grounded before entering back into the outside world. Have your client stand and breathe deeply, walk around, go to the bathroom, drink water or tea and advise them to eat a high protein meal as soon as possible. Then work out an adequate maintenance plan.

It is also a nice practice to burn cedar and sage (see Other Cleansing and Recharging Techniques, page 173) or a high quality incense and surround your client's aura with the purifying fragrance before leaving your environment. This will also clear the air before your next client arrives and refreshen your healing space.

CHAPTER VI
MAINTENANCE: PERSONAL RESPONSIBIILTY FOR THE HEALING PROCESS

When a crystal healing is completed it is important to spend time working with your client to set up a personal maintenance program. This is one of the most significant aspects of the healing process. During crystal healings very deep and sacred sources within are accessed, laying the foundation for change to occur. But the vitality of the experience is lost and becomes only a memory if it is not actively incorporated into personal daily practice. Just as the psychic surgeons in the Philippines can remove the physical illness from the body, the dis-ease usually reoccurs if the correlating mental and emotional habits are not also changed.

Crystal Healing

The idea is to assist each individual in tapping their own internal resources instead of becoming dependent on you as the healer or even upon the crystals. Sometimes it is necessary to lean upon others until we are strong enough to stand on our own. The role of the crystal healer is to "be there" and assist the healing process. But true empowerment comes when the individual personally claims the light and learns how to use it in daily life. This personal responsibility for the healing process allows it to become a reality. It takes constant conscious effort and daily disciplinary action to incorporate the changes that have occurred on the subtle levels of the subconscious and superconscious.

An important factor in grounding the reality that is witnessed and experienced during crystal healings is dependent upon the stones that are used at the first, second and third chakras in the layouts. When Citrine, Rutilated Quartz or Golden Topaz (see The Navel Connection, page 182) are placed on or around the umbilicus, the physical systems will infiltrate the golden energies of the crown into the navel chakra. Golden Tiger's Eye at the navel is a grounding and stabilizing force that greatly assists in the assimilation of higher frequencies into the body. Carnelian, Garnet or Bloodstone at the second center will stimulate creativity and purify the physical system in order to integrate the higher frequencies of the upper chakras and channel that creative energy throughout the chakra system. Dark Green or Black Tourmaline, Smoky Quartz, Black Onyx or Hawk's Eye placed at the groin points, knees and feet will channel the spiritual consciousness of the third eye and crown into the density of the material plane.

MEDITATION

One of the best techniques to initiate into personal practice is meditation. The preferred time for meditation is first thing in the morning to set the attitude for the day, or before retiring at night. Meditating before sleep allows the mind to release stresses that have accumulated during the day that otherwise would settle into the subconscious, creating restless sleep or the continuation of anxiety the following day. Even meditating fifteen minutes twice a day can make a remarkable difference in how you feel. Using the simple technique of following the breath through the center line will kindle the soul's response and help integrate the positive effects of the crystal healing. Inhaling and visualizing green entering into dis-eased or blocked areas while exhaling old congested thoughts or feelings will perpetuate the continuation of the healing process. Personal meditations can also be used—what is most important is that dedicated time and quiet space is given to the internalization of awareness and conscious attunement to the vision of wellness.

When time bridging is done in crystal healings and the adult returns to the child (or the present identity connects with the past or future self) it is important in the maintenance program that you continue to check in on, nourish, and integrate the alter-self into the adult reality. Revisualize the scene and frequently return to care for and nurture the child in order to make the healing complete.

A simple effective meditation that can be easily applied to assist in grounding the subtle effects of crystal healing sessions into practical reality is done with two natural Smoky Quartz generators. Sitting up straight in a

chair with the feet flat on the floor, still the mind by mentally following the flow of the breath. Hold a Smoky
Quartz crystal in each hand with the terminations pointing down away from the body. As you breathe, feel the
power of radiant black being channeled into the first
chakra on the inhale and through the anus and out the
soles of the feet on the exhale. This mental focus will activate the base center, filling it with light and fertilizing and
nourishing the seeds that were planted during the crystal
healing. After 11 minutes of the Smoky Quartz meditation
it is then beneficial to direct attention to other forms of
maintenance, i.e., affirmations, conscious reprogramming, etc.

AFFIRMATIONS

Repeating affirmations out loud is very effective in a personal maintenance program. Create images of the self as
it chooses to be and bring the words into the present tense
by saying "I am" instead of "I will be." This assists in
making the changes exist now in the present instead of
somewhere off in the future. The affirmations used
should be in direct relationship to experiences and transformations that occurred in the crystal healing session.
For example, if someone was actively working on releasing anger and resentment towards mom, the affirmation
could be:

> *"I am fulfilled in the love and nurturing of
> myself, for myself. I understand and forgive my
> mother for her inability to fulfill my needs. I now
> send to her my love and thank her for serving my
> process and teaching me the lesson of
> forgiveness."*

As this affirmation is sincerely repeated and sinks into

the subconscious, it will contain more and more genuine substance and create the thought patterns necessary to change old mental and emotional tracks that would otherwise play themselves out subconsciously and uncontrollably in your life.

INDIVIDUAL WORK
WITH
CRYSTALS AND STONES

Whatever specific crystals and stones were most effective during the crystal healing can be incorporated into personal practice. If the session revolved around self love, Rose Quartz could be used, or if you were working on the power to manifest results in life, use Citrine, etc. These stones can then be used by the recipient of the healing to wear, hold, carry, or meditate with in their private time. They can also be placed upon the body over the associated chakra areas as the person lies down and initiates their own healing.

Projector crystals can be programmed with thoughts and images of the desired result to amplify the effects of the healing (see *Crystal Enlightenment, Vol. I*, Programmed Projector Crystals, page 72). When crystals are worked with in this way it is possible to create effects that otherwise might take a much longer time because the crystal, once it is programmed, will continue to beam the positive projection into the causal plane to manifest the physical results much more quickly. Caution must be used when programming crystals in this way. The individual must be prepared to receive whatever is projected into the crystal and only the most positive thought forms should ever be programmed into crystals.

One of the best stones to use to ground positive effects in a personal maintenance plan is Black or Dark Green Tourmaline. What often appears as Black Tourmaline is in reality a dark, dark green which grounds the healing essence of green into the depth of the first chakra. This is a perfect stone to wear, carry, meditate with or hold when integrating the subtle effects of a crystal healing into daily action. Dark Tourmaline channels spiritual forces onto the earth and is a most comforting friend in times of transition, assisting to neutralize neurotic habit patterns and replace them with conscious action.

CONSCIOUS REPROGRAMMING

Through continual practice it is possible to consciously deprogram old mental tapes and reprogram into the mind that which will serve the conscious will. This practice is one that involves dedication and daily consistency. Once aware of a mental habit that is no longer productive, choose what is preferred and superimpose it over the old tape. To do this, sit quietly in a comfortable position, holding one of your favorite crystals to the third eye. Visualize yourself feeling, seeing, breathing, and acting out the new sequence. Affirm it in the present tense verbally and bring it into reality as you go through the day, consciously replacing the old mentality and associated attitudes and feelings with the chosen alternative.

If you are very shy, introverted and afraid to be around people, tune into a Citrine crystal and see yourself as feeling confident, secure, and then showering that love onto others. Visualize flowing interaction with all sorts of people, from the gas station attendant to the most personal relationships. Having this new image previously set firmly in the mind and affirmed, it is much easier to switch mental tracks in the midst of the day's activity. With the program preset and infused with the will, the physical manifestation of the chosen outcome is facilitated and life changes accordingly. This conscious reprogramming process gives power back into the hands of the individual as it enables one to change habitual tendencies and heal the heart.

When the will is consciously focused and directed it is possible to tap into an infinite source of energy and channel it into healing any aspect of the self. Each one of us has access to this source of soul force within us, and can use it to clear the mind, heal the heart, and balance the body. When the thoughts, feelings, and actions come into alignment with the spirit personal identification becomes more than just a body, a mind, or a feeling. We then know ourselves to be part of a much greater scheme of things and can usher into our lives and onto the planet the health and well being that we come to know ourselves to be.

PART II
THE MASTER CRYSTALS

CHAPTER VII
THE MASTER CRYSTALS

The Master Crystals are just that—"masters." They exist in a state of perfected form, manifesting alignment with the source of light. Each one of the Master Crystals demonstrates specific principles and opens the doorways through which entrance into the world of integrated spirit and earth can be experienced. These crystals are messengers from the heavens and teachers of divine law. Some are ruthless in stripping away the darkness of egocentric attitudes and identifications, while others serve to open conscious communication into the realms of higher self.

The Master Crystals are all teacher crystals (see *Crystal Enlightenment, Vol. I*, Page 68). The emergence of these crystals at this time and the understanding of how to use them indicates that we are ready to receive vast knowledge that we are now ready to comprehend. As a race of beings, it is possible to incorporate into our thought processes ideas and concepts that we are now capable of grasping. We only use one-tenth of our brain power. We are capable of using one hundred percent. The Master Crystals transmit frequencies which activate the higher powers of the mind and direct our attention to the soul level. More and more of the Master Crystals are being located and midwifed onto the surface of the earth to be attracted to the people that are eager and ready to make a phenomenal transformation.

The geometric constructs on the Channeling, Transmitter, and Window Crystals are their most distinguishing marks. They are symbolically profound, numerologically significant, and physically a statement of divine order. The geometry on these Master Crystals is precise and specific, determining their purpose and use. The Laser Wands and Earthkeepers are tools empowered with the ancient knowledge from the root civilizations, while the Elestial Quartz purges through the darkness of the mind, enabling the revelation of truth and attunement to the celestial realms.

The Master Crystals are most often used in personal meditation or with a partner or group of like-mindedness and intention. It is best not to have other people touch these crystals during the time period in which you are actively working with them. Each crystal will communicate its essence and function, so the clear receptivity of the individuals working with the crystals is essential to the knowledge being transmitted. Therefore, the ability to still the random thoughts that constantly arise from the subconscious and discipline the mind to receive the Master Crystal's teaching is the first lesson. By training the mind to perceive the Master Crystal's frequency the art of inter-dimensional communication is learned and the gap between human and mineral forms will be bridged.

The Master Crystals

To date I am only aware of six (of I believe twelve) of the Master Crystals, and they are all Clear Quartz. The rest have not revealed themselves to me at this time. Perhaps they will by the time *Volume III* emerges; or perhaps you will discover them. What is exciting is that we are ready for the ones that are now manifest and they are ready to be activated by our conscious attunement to them. Use these crystals with absolute respect and purity of intention. They are our guides, they are our teachers, they are our friends, they are here. Are you ready?!

CHAPTER VIII

CHANNELING CRYSTALS

GEOMETRIC AND
NUMEROLOGICAL SIGNIFICANCE

Channeling crystals can be recognized by a large seven-sided face in the front center of the crystal with the opposing back side manifesting a perfect triangle. Along with the triangle, there are usually other smaller crystals projecting out of the back side.

Numerologically, seven is a metaphysical number symbolic of the student, the mystic, and the seeker of deeper truth. Seven represents the intuition of the higher mind and the one who goes within to find wisdom. Seven is the number of mystical truths that are realized when detachment is attained enabling third eye vision. The large seven sided configuration that the channeling crystals so obviously demonstrate is the doorway through which inner truth can be revealed.

The three-sided triangle on the back of the crystal allows for those truths to be verbally spoken. The number three represents the power of speech and the ability to creatively and joyously express. The powerful combination of the seven takes the mind within to find the wisdom. The three enables that to be manifested and shared through the spoken word. (Much of the information that I have personally received concerning the power and potential of crystals was received with a channeling crystal before I ever knew that there was such a thing.)

The large seven-sided face represents the seven qualities that the human consciousness must attain in order to access and channel the wisdom of the soul. Each one of the lines comprising the septagon represents one of the virtues in balance and in harmony with the other six. These are: love, knowledge, freedom, manifestation (the ability to project and create), joy, peace, and unity. When these virtues are integrated into one's being the door to channeling truth is opened and wisdom flows forth.

THE USE AND POTENTIAL MISUSE OF CHANNELING

The word "channeling" is being used frequently today, and means different things in different circles. In reference to the Channeling Master Crystals it means channeling and expressing the source of truth and wisdom from the depth of the soul. It means conscious connection to the ultimate source of knowledge within the self.

Channeling is something that can be potentially abused. Many people are channeling today. Many sources are being contacted and much varied information is being accessed. There is tremendous sensationalism revolving around channeling, and oftentimes it can be an ego trap. Many out-of-the-body souls wish to use physical vehicles to express themselves. These discarnate entities may or may not be more evolved and have clearer access to knowledge than the person they choose to speak through. The information may or may not be pertinent or correct. Caution must be taken when receiving a channeling or becoming a channel. Do not give your power over to a force unless you know beyond a shadow of a doubt that it's intentions are pure and it will serve your highest good. I would suggest that before channeling sessions the channel and the receiver sit down together and call upon protection and guidance using personal techniques to surround each other in light or affirming the decree described on page 16 (Chapter II, Preparation). This will ensure the proper dissemination of information from the highest possible source.

If a person opens up their psychic channels to an entity that is less evolved than themselves, their own vital energy can be usurped and they often feel very tired and disoriented afterwards. If a person wants to be channeled to and opens up their subconscious to an entity that they assume knows more about them than they know about themselves, they can be severely misguided if that source is off track. If one's mind is opened and receives untrue advice and believes it, their own intuitive forces are stifled and they base their reality on what someone else perceives rather than looking within to their own source of power and knowing. This is not to say that there are not reliable sources of discarnate entities available to assist us in our process. The point is that we all have the knowledge within ourselves if we look in the right places, and it is possible to attain information from our own infinite source and channel that wisdom into our lives.

CHANNELING CRYSTALS

Undoubtedly there are many high souls that we can draw strength from in times of need and align our consciousness with in order to receive knowledge and light. There are spiritual guides that are ever present with us to assist in our evolutionary process, and forces that we can call upon for protection and guidance. But where our true strength and wisdom lies is within ourselves, and the more that source is attuned to, the more personal security and empowerment evolve.

The Channeling Crystals are here to teach us how to tap into the wisdom within ourselves. They represent through their sacred geometry, associated virtues and numerological symbology, the ability to go within our own source, access truth, and then bring that forth through verbal expression. These crystals have arrived on the scene to teach us how to gain and channel our own light from the purest, truest depths of our souls. Sometimes in that process we can (and often do) encounter other entities that can be acknowledged and learned from. The difference is that we are not giving our power away, and the affirmation or disagreement of information is always checked with our own inner touchstone. As we confirm our own wisdom in this way we learn how to draw upon our personal resources to guide us in our lives.

THE ART OF USING CHANNELING CRYSTALS

Channeling Crystals can be used for many purposes. They are tools in personal meditation practices to gain inner clarity and channel the light of wisdom into the mind and into daily affairs. They can be used when specific answers to specific questions are needed, or when you want to gain information in a particular area. Channeling Crystals are great partners to work with to retrieve record keeper information, or in conjunction with Transmitter Crystals. They can be used in group circles or in work with another person. In either of these cases the conscious intention of what information is to be received should be agreed upon by all persons involved. This conscious mental linking allows for the group (or persons) to unite their minds at the same source to perceive desired information.

Before actually working with the Channeling Crystal, hold it in the left hand and quiet the mind by mentally following the flow of the breath. Meditate upon the seven principals, bring them into mental focus, and identify with them. Visualize a pure blue light around the throat chakra and a deep purple ray at the third eye. Other crystals and stones may be used to assist in activating these centers—Aquamarine, Indicolite, Blue Celestite, Gem Silica for the throat chakra, and Amethyst, Fluorite or Luvulite for the third eye. These stones may be worn, held, previously meditated with or laid upon the associated points to assist the intuitive powers of the third eye vision and verbal expression from the throat. After activating these two chakras, verbally call upon the light and wisdom of your soul to come forth and guide, protect and inform you.

After clearing, quieting and consciously programming the mind, one of two different approaches can be taken. The first is to hold the seven-sided face to the third eye center and breathe long and deep while you focus within. The second method is to place the index finger and thumb of each hand together, connecting the wisdom of the Jupiter (index) finger to that of the personal ego identification (the thumb). Then bring the index finger

CHANNELING CRYSTALS

and the thumb of the right hand to touch the same of the left, keeping the rest of the fingers straight. Place this mudra on the apex of the termination of the Channeling Crystal, close your eyes, and allow the mind to be very still, open, and receptive.

Whatever impressions, symbols, images, or feelings are received once the Channeling Crystals are at work, acknowledge and express without doubt or distrust. The impressions may be vague or subtle at first, but once the mind adjusts itself to the frequency of the Channeling Crystal it will flow through without hesitation. Allow the information to come through you without intellectualizing or thinking about it. It is a good idea to tape each channeling session, have someone else take notes, or write it down immediately afterwards. Even though you are totally conscious, the state of mind being accessed is altered, oftentimes unfamiliar and not always easily recalled from memory.

As attunement is made and refined, it is possible to sense other beings present that hold certain knowledge. If you feel that you could be served by communicating with them, you can consciously choose to link your mind with theirs and receive the transmission of information. If channeling out loud during this time the voice may change in nature as you align your consciousness with theirs. If this occurs, I would suggest that you maintain a clear strong connection to your own source of light and maintain your identity while simultaneously allowing the expression of the other entity.

In the process of allowing discarnate entities to assist, it is important to not empower the other source as being the ultimate authority. Instead, see that entity as being a part of yourself (of your oversoul) and being connected to the same source of light that you are. The benefit in allowing other entities (voices) to come through is it allows you to disassociate from your own linear identity and see yourself as a part of a much greater whole. The intention of Channeling Crystals is to teach personal empowerment by enabling one to channel all of the different facets and all of the various rays that exist within each person.

There are a few Channeling Crystals that have been programmed by advanced beings and the ancient Elders of our race. These crystals are for particular people who will attract them into their lives and know that they have work to do with them. Only those who are meant to receive information from these crystals will be capable of aligning their minds to the frequency of the crystal to activate them. As they do, very specific information will be revealed and channeled through. These specialized programmed channeling crystals usually have clouded inclusions, spiraling whisps, phantoms or record keeper markings (see *Crystal Enlightenment, Vol. I*, pages 65 & 75). These are unique channeling crystals and are usually large and breathtaking. The other more commonly found channeling crystals will serve their human partners to align with and clearly channel the wisdom of their souls to answer any questions or ponderings.

CHAPTER IX
TRANSMITTER CRYSTALS

GEOMETRIC AND NUMEROLOGICAL
SYMBOLOGY

Transmitter Crystals are also known by the geometry of their faces. They too manifest the seven:three ratio (as does the Channeling Crystal). However, in Transmitter Crystals a perfect triangle is in the center of the crystal connected by two symmetrical seven-sided faces on both sides of the triangle. The seven represents the ability to control the physical senses and desires in order to realize the truth with the superconscious mind. Seven is the God-realized self, and the three brings that through the individual consciousness to be personally expressed and manifested.

The numerological combination of seven-three-seven symbolically indicates personal empowerment and manifestation (the three) held in balance by the pair of sevens which directly connects to the superconsciousness. The very act of blending the superconsciousness with the individual consciousness grounds into the earth a way to take universal knowledge and wisdom and make it work in day to day life.

The center triangle is the connecting point, the bridge between personal and universal identification and represents unity. The seven-sided faces embody the virtues of God-enlightened beings which, again, are: love, knowledge, freedom, manifestation, joy, peace, and unity.

Through the use of Transmitter Crystals it is possible to connect the conscious mind to universal wisdom and receive specific information pertaining to individual circumstance or to attain cosmic truth (depending upon the intent).

REFINING COMMUNICATION

Transmitter Crystals, when used properly, can transmit human thought forms into the universal mind to be received and responded to accordingly. The first lesson that Transmitter Crystals teach is the art of refining one's communication. When thoughts or questions are clearly defined and projected into a Transmitter Crystal, it will beam those mental vibrations out into the universe to be acutely replied to. If a person is unclear, uncentered or unable to clarify one's own thoughts, what comes back will also be scattered. Such is the way of the universe. If one is precise and exact in stating to the universe what is wanted, the return answer will reflect that clarity. One of the main elements in communication is being able to put

TRANSMITTER CRYSTAL

out precisely what you feel you need in order to come into wholeness. The other equally important aspect is being able and feeling worthy to receive it when it returns.

To a large degree our thoughts become the mental blueprint that creates our own personal physical reality. We have what we already transmitted into the universe. If we don't have what we want, it could be because we have not explicitly defined and transmitted our intentions clearly. It could also be that we have not been capable of integrating into our lives the effects of our positive thought projections. As one works with Transmitter Crystals it is possible to learn the art of communication by clearly stating your intentions with the assurance that you are ready and willing to incorporate the return energy.

The Transmitter Crystals are a check and balance system—if you don't get back a clear answer it means that either you have not been detailed enough in stating the question or projection, or you need to be more open and receptive in order to receive the answer. Transmitter Crystals are great teachers in helping us clarify what we want, in assisting us to develop the ability to project that intention out into the universe, and enabling us to receive the reciprocal response.

USING TRANSMITTER CRYSTALS

Transmitter Crystals can work in a couple of different ways. In either case you are consciously sending thoughts or questions out in order to receive a direct response. The first and most often used method is to connect and align one's mind to the universal mind. (This technique is very similar to using programmed projector crystals—see *Crystal Enlightenment, Vol. I*, page 72). The other way is to consciously set up communication with out-of-the-body spiritual guides and master teachers. In either case the intention should be clearly defined and stated.

Because of the ability Transmitter Crystals have to transmit energy from the earth plane into the higher dimensions, these crystals can be used as communication bases to establish conscious connection with other life forms. The Transmitter Crystals are learning devices through which one can further develop intuitive faculties and telepathic communication. They can also be used between two people to send and receive messages. Once the information has been received by the appropriate receptor the transmission is completed and the crystal is emptied of the thought form. This serves as a self-protective device.

Before programming these crystals with your thoughts, take some time and sit quietly, breathe deeply, and bring into conscious focus the virtues that the seven sides represent. Align with those spiritual attributes while you hold the Transmitter Crystal in your left hand. Then clearly define the question in your mind, place the triangle up to your third eye, and mentally project the inquiry into the Transmitter Crystal. Then place the crystal on an altar or in a special place and leave undisturbed for twenty four hours. During this time, when transmission is occurring, the crystals need to be in an upright position. If they do not have a natural flat base to stand up on their own, they will need to be propped, preferably with wood. Do not use another crystal or stones to prop them, as this could interfere with transmission. During this twenty four hour period, as much natural light (sunlight, moonlight,

TRANSMITTER CRYSTAL

etc.) as the Transmitter Crystal can be exposed to will facilitate the projective power of the crystal. At preferably the same time the following day, again sit quietly, align with the seven attributes, and then completely still your mind and become very open, receptive, and willing. Again place the triangle to the brow and receive the information that has been relayed back to you. The most ideal time to program Transmitter Crystals is at either sunrise or sunset when the light forces are dramatically shifting and the ethers are most open.

During the time that you are working directly with Transmitter Crystals, it is best not to let anyone else touch them, as their vibrations could interfere with your energies that have been set into the crystal. Also, after the transmission the crystal should be cleansed (see Sun and Water Method, *Crystal Enlightenment, Vol. I*, page 28).

These crystals are powerful forces when consciously set. They can potentially connect the human consciousness to realms where celestial entities exist. In this dimension there is no duality, only light and the conscious expression of light. The beings that exist in this dimension do not know what dualistic polarity living is like. In establishing conscious communication with them, we on earth can receive the light that is constant in their reality to assist us in maintaining our own stable connection to the source, even though we live in a world of half day and half night. They, in return for sending their light, learn what it is like to live in a reality where the light force is not continually present and must be found within the Self, which requires faith, trust, and mastery. Working together through the Transmitter Crystals, each breed of being gains greater experience, knowledge, and advancement. This type of inter-dimensional communication also assists immensely in bridging the light of consciousness throughout the universe.

BALANCED POLARITIES

Transmitter Crystals and Channeling Crystals are polarities. The Transmitter is the male, the yang, the projector and the assertive. The Channeling Crystals are female, yin, and the receptor. Yet each of these crystals unto themselves are balanced polarities. The Transmitter Crystals project out thought forms, yet also have the ability to receive, hold, and retain information. The Channeling Crystals guide the awareness within to perceive the truth, yet are also capable of projecting it out through the voice in order for wisdom to be clearly received. Each of these Master Crystals are great teachers in the art of communication, demonstrating the ability to give as well as receive. They exemplify mental clarity, conscious focus, and projection while simultaneously manifesting receptivity and perception.

It is possible to find both channeling faculties as well as the transmitter qualities embodied in the same crystal. These specialized crystals manifest perfect geometry with the six faces comprising the termination alternating between triangles and seven-sided figures. The ratio of these crystals is 7:3:7:3:7:3, with the triangle marking the back face of the Channeling Crystal being the same triangle in the center of the Transmitter Crystal. They have been fondly named "the Dow Crystals," being discovered by Jane Ann Dow. These very unique and rare crystals are indeed masters of communication and extremely powerful forces to work with, incorporating both channeling and transmitting characteristics.

If you choose to work with either Transmitter Crystals, Channeling Crystals, or the Dow Crystals, keep your eyes open and put out the beam for one, or program one of your programmed projector crystals (see *Crystal Enlightenment, Vol. I*, page 72), and start noticing the specific geometry of the crystals you encounter. Also, check your private collection. There may already be one there, awaiting activation through your conscious attunement to it.

CHAPTER X
THE WINDOW CRYSTALS

RECOGNIZING
A TRUE WINDOW
CRYSTAL

Window Crystals are recognized by a large diamond-shaped window in the center of the crystal. The window actually becomes the seventh face with the four points of the diamond intersecting with the other main angles of the crystal. In other words, the top point of the diamond connects with the line leading directly up to the termination, the side points connect with angles forming opposing faces, and the bottom point leads to the termination running down to the base of the crystal (see photo).

Window Crystals are distinguished from regular diamond-faced crystals in that the window is clear and big enough to see into the inner world of the crystal. In Window Crystals the diamond is large enough in relationship to the faces comprising the termination to be considered

WINDOW CRYSTAL

a face in and of itself, creating a crystal with seven faces instead of six. This empowers the Window Crystal with a dimension of being not known among other members of the quartz family.

Regular diamond-faced crystals, which are more commonly found, are not all Window Crystals. The diamonds on diamond-faced crystals are smaller and usually found on the side angles (not in the center front, as in Window Crystals) and are a side attraction rather than the main event. Diamond-faced crystals are in the same family as Window Crystals, but are not of the same dimension or power. If you have to wonder if it is a Window Crystal, it isn't. The window will be apparent and obvious.

The four sides of the diamond in the Window Crystal represent the bridging of the upper and lower worlds as the two triangular shapes meet at common points. This allows for clear vision into the deeper spiritual meaning of physical reality. The diamond shape symbolizes the balance and integration between the higher and the lower, the inner and the outer, the spiritual and the physical.

MASTERS OF REFLECTION

Window Crystals are like open windows into the realm of the soul through which one can see beyond illusionary identities and into the essence of the Self. They will reflect the soul, and in doing so often mirror the darker shadows of fear and insecurity that inhibit the soul's expression of light. In this way they become very powerful teachers. They are like gurus in that their reflection

WINDOW CRYSTAL

is so clear that they simply return the image of yourself. Window Crystals are empty and egoless, and provide a means through which one can see into the deeper regions of being.

The Window Crystal is a very personal crystal and grows in power the more it is used. They very easily become personal meditation partners as they make you want to go inside, be quiet, and witness yourself. Window Crystals will directly reflect the individual that is consciously working with them. These crystals are such clear receptors of energy that they will immediately shine back into the human consciousness that which they receive. Window Crystals do not hold impressions or carry records within them. They reflect. If you see something in a Window Crystal that you do not like, it can't be blamed on the last person that gazed into it. It is you, or some aspect of yourself that needs to be looked at. Wherever you are at in relation to yourself you will see as you gaze into the Window Crystal. They will reflect all of a person's light back to them just as they will reflect the shadows of the subconscious. They are honest. They do not discriminate which parts to reflect back. They simply reflect what is there. Just as there are many types of glass but only one kind that is mirror, the Window Crystal is unique and specialized in its field.

There are not many Window Crystals around. In all my years of working with crystals, I have only seen a few. They can, however, be attracted if one is willing to honestly look very clearly at oneself. In order to incorporate what the Window Crystals will reflect, one must be willing to let go of thoughts, actions, patterns, and behaviors that prevent the acceptance of responsibility to live in the truth. Otherwise conflict can arise in one's life by having seen the soul's potential yet being unable or unwilling to manifest it.

HOW TO USE WINDOW CRYSTALS

There are two main ways that Window Crystals can be used. The first is to still the mind and then fix a steady gaze through the window into the inside of the crystal. In this way Window Crystals are similar to working with crystal balls (see *Crystal Enlightenment, Vol. I*, page 74), in that the window will reflect into the mind the colors, impressions and feelings of the auric body. The more one works with Window Crystals in this way the easier it will be to perceive the subtle impressions that will appear to the mind's eye when a focused stare is directed into the diamond shape. The diamond face expands the perspective as the very nature of the diamond is to sparkle and reflect. Often when people gaze into the diamond window they see an unlimited number of diamonds expanding out, which connects their consciousness to a sense of infinity.

The other way in which Window Crystals can be used is by closing the eyes and placing the diamond face up to the brow. Window Crystals are very visual. As you hold the window to your third eye they will show you pictures. In this way they can be used to assist you to look within a particular aspect of yourself, of a situation, or of a relationship. Before using Window Crystals to reflect on specifics, first clear your mind and then bring into mental focus the specific aspect in which you choose to find greater perspective. Present that image into the window and then again clear the mind and look within.

Whether Window Crystals are used to gaze into or placed to the third eye depends on the person using them and the individual situation. If you choose to work with

126

these crystals, try both methods and see which works best for you.

There are several ways that Window Crystals can be used outside of personal meditations. They can be used to read another person's aura by placing the window towards the person and then turning it to your third eye. Window Crystals can also be used in this way to help define another person's soul purpose. The window will assist you in seeing the interims between lifetimes when decisions were made on what experiences were needed to fulfill the individual's destiny. The linking with this pure soul energy enables one to see into the past as well as the future to discover one's true purpose. Just as one looks through a window to see that which is on the other side, when one looks through a Window Crystal it is possible to see into the inner workings of things and come to know the unseen reality behind events. When using these crystals in work with other people in this way, it is very important to clear your own mind and center yourself beforehand so that you, like the Window Crystal, can become a clear reflector.

Window Crystals can also be of benefit in locating missing persons by projecting a clear image of that person into the crystal and then perceiving the return images. In this way Window Crystals can be great tools for psychics who are working with the police force to help find lost children or stolen goods.

These crystals are also very powerful tools to use in death experiences when one is willing to see beyond the limitations of the physical body and wants to consciously prepare to enter into the world of spirit. Through work with Window Crystals at this most sensitive and transitory time, it is possible to ease the turmoil of physical pain by attuning the mind to the soul level and focusing beyond the material plane.

CHAPTER XI
THE ELESTIALS

A GIFT FROM THE ANGELS

The Elestial Crystals are more commonly known as skeletal quartz. These specialized quartz crystals are gifts that have been ushered onto the planet in order to assist in the mass cleansing, healing and reawakening that is occurring at this time upon the earth. With them they bring great strength, particularly strength in overcoming human emotional burdens.

The Elestials embody the very substance of the physical plane while simultaneously aligning with angelic vibrations. Their source is beyond time itself and their origin is the celestial realm. As heavenly forces were materialized into physical time and space, the Elestial Crystals embraced the four elements and were given birth. Many of them appear singed as they bear the fire element and often turn a true smoky color. They are the purest of the physical plane emerging out of the womb of

ELESTIAL

the mother earth and being transported through the ethers into the atmosphere, they represent the air. Usually growing separate from other quartz crystals, they are mined in or close to water sources and often resemble solution quartz, and frequently are found with water bubbles inside.

Carrying the knowledge of the pre-physical state, the Elestials become great comforters to those who are in the dying process, assisting one to release the fears of leaving the physical body in order to identify with the immortality of the soul. Also being born of the earth, they assist in the assimilation of the vital earth elements in order to be nurtured and nourished by this planet, bringing about a sense of balance and well being, particularly to those who are not native to this world.

ELESTIAL CHARACTERISTICS

The Elestial Crystals (called the El's for short) are unlike any other quartz configuration. They are naturally terminated over the body of the crystal, generally having no dulled or broken faces. This allows for an incredible radiance as light reflects off of all of the natural faces. Unlike regular quartz, the Elestial Crystals may have several terminated points on a single piece or may be a single terminated piece or may have no terminated apexes.

The most distinguishing characteristic of these crystals is the fact that they are etched and layered with markings. Bringing into skeletal form the entirety of primal life stuff, the Elestials bear geometric patterns and constructs which in and of themselves state profound laws of the universe. It is as if the symbols of a cosmic alphabet have been written and formed in these crystals. When held in the right hand, with a stilled, attuned and open mind, while running the index finger of the left hand over the etching, it is possible to align with the source of knowledge and interpret the universal language not yet known to the human mind.

The language that the Elestials communicate is one of supreme knowledge. They represent the higher mind of humankind and many of them even resemble brain tissue. The combination of the highly charged quartz material with the layered etching draws the mind within itself, allowing for the discovery and eventual identification with cosmic consciousness. When looking into Elestial Quartz layer upon layer of inner dimension can be seen within the body of the crystal. Simply by gazing into these crystals and then closing your eyes, you have the means to go deeper within your own being because the inner matrix of the crystal will register subliminally to the subconscious mind as a door or a gateway into the depths of the self.

These crystals stabilize brain wave frequencies and neutralize erratic confused thought forms. When this occurs the crown chakra is activated and the pineal gland secretes, resulting in an expanded state of awareness. As the mind stabilizes into a neutral state the frequencies of the angelic realm can be infiltrated.

The nature of the El's is to take one deep within the self, to connect with that which is the innermost truth, the source and the foundation for existence. In the process many of the old identifications must fall by the wayside and be laid to rest in peace. The El's represent the mind of one who can harmonize with the higher self, and in doing so links with the very source of cosmic power. The power of the El's lies in their ability to communicate to the mind that which is sure, secure and true. These frequencies may or may not be easy to identify with. If a person is used to thinking of himself as being physically beautiful and has built up a strong identification around that image, the El's may show him that in the larger scope of things the physical appearance is but a meager shadow of what he really is. That shadow image of the self may not be easy to swallow, or the idea of the self being grander than form may be difficult to accommodate. But the truth of the matter remains. These crystals will take you to the core of the matter, to the truth, to the bottom line skeletal foundation of the self. The Elestials usually emerge into one's life at a time when the internal rooting into one's basic essence is about to occur. If you find yourself with one, welcome it as a friend, for it is. A friend that will assist you in accessing the deepest source of your own angelic nature.

INITIATING PURIFICATION

When heavy laden with emotional stress it is very difficult to think clearly, behave rationally, or express the virtues of the higher self. Many emotional habits are formed early in life and carried on into adult behavior and attitudes can be so subtle as to make one believe that it is the present situation that is being responded to. In fact, it is often a deeply ingrained emotional pattern that can be played out over and over again with different people and different circumstances. These emotional bonds can be broken with the help of the Elestial Crystals. The El's with their multi-faceted nature, ingrained depth, and gridwork markings are tools which can be used to clear the heart of emotional burdens and direct the energy to the crown chakra for cosmic enlightenment.

There is a caution and an awareness to be practiced in the use of these crystals. They are very powerful and one should have full knowledge of their effects before using them in crystal healings with other people. The skeletal element of these crystals will strip away anything that is not in harmony and attunement with the frequency of the crown chakra. The Elestials seek to neutralize the random ordering of thoughts and feelings in order to bring the consciousness into alignment with the highest energy center in the human body. In doing so, they can work much like Black Obsidian, Malachite or Azurite in that they will surface what needs to be dealt with and cleansed, bringing into acute awareness that which is preventing one from experiencing truth. It is not that the crystals in and of themselves are necessarily purgers, but if there is cleansing that needs to be done they will purify to the depths of being. It is not uncommon for one who has worked intensively with Elestial Crystals to have thoughts and feelings arise from the subconscious that have been considered long since processed and released. On the other hand, if a person is totally clear and centered the El's will open the crown center and initiate the connection, communication and integration of celestial forms.

Before embarking on an Elestial experience it is important to ask oneself, "Am I willing to see and know the truth?" For these crystals represent the truth laid bare and will clear all outer elements of personality and ego. If worked with properly the Elestials can completely change the quality of one's life. Thoughts of self-importance and self concern can no longer exist when working with these crystals. The larger the crystal the more light it will reflect, the more powerful it is, and the more energy it will have to strike down that which is not real. The energy emitted from these crystals can be devastating if one is not fully ready to acknowledge the truth.

The cleansing process that the Elestials initiate can be traumatic if one is not prepared and they should be used with the utmost awareness. If one is confused or emotionally imbalanced these crystals will amplify and magnify those feelings, and the effects could be severe and radical if one is not ready or able to process the inevitable changes that will occur. The Elestials should only be used in crystal healing layouts with permission and awareness of the receiver as to the potential of the healing crisis that can result. With consent they can then be used at the center of the chest, at the third eye center, or at top of the head to clear the heart chakra and focus energy at the crown. It is of added benefit to use Green Tourmaline around the heart and Blue Tourmaline around the third eye in conjunction with the Elestials when used in crystal healing layouts. As the clearing occurs and the illumination evolves, the Tourmaline will assist the assimilation of the higher forces into the body and strengthen the nervous system, enabling the physical vehicle to embody the increased flux of spirit force.

BALANCING MIND AND HEART

When the Elestials are held, meditated with, or placed upon the body they will first bring into view that which needs to be cleared and then usher the mind into a rational state. Achieving mental balance, the illusions that bind the mind to the world of the senses are penetrated and

ELESTIAL

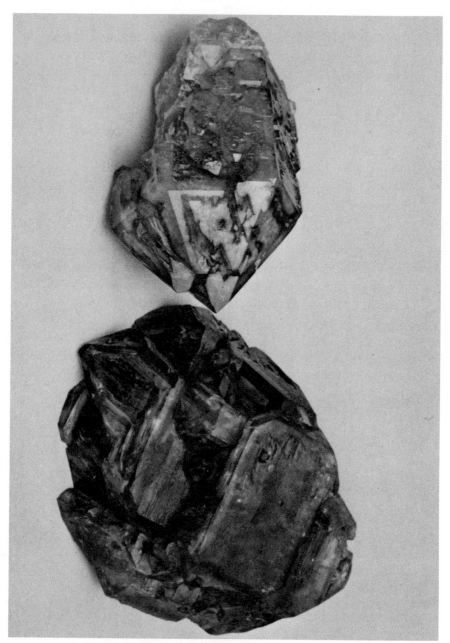

the veils of confusion are lifted. This calm, centered state of mind is brought about as the Elestials clear the mental passageways and concentrate energy at the pineal gland in the center of the brain. It is as if all extraneous thoughts and feelings are brought into sharp focus at the top of the head. Experiencing mental and emotional peace, it is then possible to view the thoughts and feelings that can habitually imbalance one's life. Observing from a detached perspective, personal power can be gained and conscious reprogramming can be done (See Conscious Reprogramming, Chapter 6, page 92).

Stepping outside of the emotions to look at them objectively, it becomes apparent that it is often our own self judgment of our real feelings that is the culprit, and not the feeling itself. Feelings in and of themselves are the heart's natural response to life. E-motions arise when we do not put into motion our true feelings in the moment that we experience them. In the true expression of feelings, they are felt, expressed, and released in the moment that they arise, whether the feeling is anger, joy or sorrow. E-motions occur when that spontaneous response to life is judged, held back, or stifled by our personal condemnation about it or our concern over what others might think about us if we act ourselves. Emotions are feelings with turmoil attached to them.

Because the Elestial Crystals originate in realms unaffected by human emotion, they can be great teachers in assisting us to understand the true nature of our feelings and stabilize our natural expression of them. This crystal is therefore very beneficial for people who have suppressed their real thoughts and feelings or who are emotionally hypersensitive.

As we learn to express our feelings in the moment that we feel them, and in so doing release the charge, we

137

will be capable of keeping our hearts open and our minds clear. Balancing rational perspective with emotional sensitivity, the heart and the mind become good friends and the angelic qualities of the soul find expression through both.

APPLYING ELESTIAL ENERGIES

The Elestials are a rare breed of crystal serving multipurposes. The innate depth that they contain takes one within and like stripping away layer upon layer of an onion, they cleanse that which is preventing illumination. Then, neutralizing the mind and bringing about a clear rational perspective, the crown chakra is opened as the Elestials invite you in to the lighted center core of your own inner being.

These are very powerful crystals and depending upon the individual's state of awareness, will work differently. If someone needs to cleanse, they will strip away ego traits and bring into sharp focus personality flaws. If another person is clear and centered they will serve to open the crown chakra. It is the responsibility of the caretakers of such crystals to be fully aware of their power and potential before using them in healing practices. I suggest that these crystals are personally worked with before using them on other people. Once aligned with their energies, apply the following guidelines before using them in crystal healings:

The Elestials

1. Tune into yourself, the crystal, and the person you are working with, and sense if it is appropriate to use the Elestial crystal.
2. Ask the person you are working with if they are willing to consciously look at, process, and take responsibility for whatever the Elestials might surface.
3. Ask permission of the person you are working with if you may use the powers of the Elestials with them. If you do not receive consent, do not use them.
4. Apply the information in Part I to clear whatever comes up.
5. Be sure to assist the recipient in working out an adequate maintenance plan to process and integrate the effects created by the Elestials.

An advanced Elestial layout that can be done when one is fully prepared for spiritual purging is as follows: Place an Elestial crystal at the top of the head, one at the third eye, and one at the heart center. Use four pieces of Green Tourmaline around the crystal at the heart and four pieces of Blue Tourmaline around the one at the brow. Place Malachite at the solar plexus, Azurite above the Elestial at the third eye, and a large piece of Black Tourmaline at the instep of each foot (for the specific effects of the following stones, see *Crystal Enlightenment, Vol. I*). Have your client breathe long and deep, focusing on the center line for no more than fifteen minutes while consciously infiltrating the energies of the stones. This layout should only be done when one is fully aware of the powers of the stones involved and is ready and willing to process the effects. The layout should not be repeated until one has thoroughly learned and integrated the lessons that will evolve from the healing.

When the mind is clear and open, Elestial quartz can also be used in conjunction with Gem Silica at the third eye to initiate powerful visionary experiences. This dynamic combination of energies can create a momentary flash of immortality, bringing petty fears and problems into perspective and showing one his/her unique individual part in the entire scheme of things.

The Elestials have been proven to be of great value in treating epilepsy and schizophrenia. Elestial quartz is also one of the best crystals to use in cases of drug related burnout. One of the effects of using psychedelic drugs is that the chemicals in the drugs cause the pineal and pituitary glands to secrete at a higher rate, creating uncommon chemical reactions in the brain which in turn creates altered, expanded states of awareness. The body is generally not capable of withstanding the hormonal and chemical effects and as a result the nervous system is weakened, brain cells are destroyed, and pineal-pituitary functioning is decreased.

Elestial quartz has been known to be of benefit in revitalizing burned out brain tissue due to drug abuse and restoring proper balance between the higher glands in the brain. (Personal research is now being conducted in this area.) With continued use of Elestial quartz (and Green Tourmaline) it is possible to rejuvenate and revitalize fatigued and overstimulated areas of the brain and nervous systems. In these circumstances place an Elestial Crystal at the base of the skull and one at the third eye center while directing a Green Tourmaline wand into cranial points. It is of added benefit to also have Black Tourmaline at the feet or the groin points to help ground the Elestial energies into the physical body.

The Elestials

The Elestial Crystals can also be used between two people who want to experience their soul connection. Sitting cross-legged with a straight spine facing one another, have one person hold the crystal in the upright palm of the left hand. The partner places their left palm face down over the crystal as each person closes their eyes and opens their mind. The images that will be seen will not only be of past or future lives together, but also of the deep connection that they have experienced through eons of time.

The Elestials are great teachers and servants to our earth. They are heart, they are mind, they are soul. They are powerful sources of light. If used properly they can open the celestial realm and integrate into our beings angelic characteristics.

CHAPTER XII
THE LASER WANDS

THE REBIRTH OF LASER WANDS

Laser Wands are inconspicuously dynamic and powerful crystals. They have been held in safekeeping within the earth since ancient days when they were used in the healing temples of Lemuria. They were laid to rest before the fall of the great Lemurian empire by the elders of that race and have been in a dormant stage until just a moment ago in our time period. The Laser Wands were stored within the sacred chambers of underground temples and are now being relocated, mostly into mines on the South American continent. The beings of inner earth have kept these crystals safe and protected and have only recently released them onto the surface of the earth to be used once again in advanced healing practices. Within these crystals lie the secret of laser ray projection. We, as a race, are only now ready to consciously use a small portion of their potential. In the wrong hands these power objects could create much damage and negative results.

In the right hands they become extremely effective healing tools and beneficial teachers.

Laser Wands carry within them the knowledge not only of the ancient root civilizations but of the stellar spaces from which they originated. These crystals have a profound and intimate relationship with both outer space and the depths of inner earth. When they are worked with by humans on the surface of the planet, they serve to create a bridge between the worlds. Often Laser Wands are in tabular form (see *Crystal Enlightenment, Vol. I*, page 62), which represents the integration, balancing, and linking together of dimensions, polarities or frequencies. When Laser Wands are used in personal meditation it is possible to bridge gaps in communion with the Self as well as establish finer communication with the crystalline kingdom.

RECOGNIZING LASER WANDS

Laser Wands look ancient and rugged. They are not necessarily attractive crystals. In fact, some of them could be defined as rather homely. That is part of their disguise. Laser Wands don't look particularly beautiful to the popular image of what "beauty" is concerning crystals. These wands must be seen by their energy. If someone is looking for only an outer surface image of perfection, they will not be attracted by these crystals. To one who has learned the truth of external appearances and has developed third eye vision, these crystals will appear to be beacons of pure light.

Laser Wands are long slender crystals with small faces comprising the termination. They resemble fingers;

the nail would be the faces forming the termination with the body being lengthy and narrow yet expanding in width at the bottom of the crystal. This tapered pine cone look distinguishes them as wands through which energy can be directed and projected.

Laser Wands often have etching or markings on them unlike any on other types of crystals. The writing on these crystals resembles hieroglyphics that entice one into deciphering the symbols that are obviously presented. These crystals, that were once used in the healing temples of Lemuria, recorded their own experiences as they gathered knowledge on the human condition and how to heal it. Therefore, the more healing that was done with these crystals, the more powerful they became, the more knowledge they contain, and the more markings can be noticed. Through personal meditation and attunement with etched Laser Wands one can virtually be educated in the advanced healing arts that were practiced by the Lemurians.

As previously mentioned, Laser Wands often resemble tabbies except that their angles are not straight. The broken crooked angles are the main distinguishing marks of Laser Wands. The angles forming the body of the crystal usually start small at the base angle of the crystal's face and expand out considerably by the time they reach the bottom of the crystal. The angles in Laser Wands are unique in that they are curved and yet still contain a direct unbroken frequency of energy. This is symbolic of the illusion of imperfect form, which is one of the main lessons that these crystals teach. Their form appears imperfect, yet they are pure in their essence, energy, and projection.

The angles on the Laser Crystals are only bent up until they reach the faces forming the termination and

LASER WAND

then they are straight. This allows for energy to move at a tremendously rapid rate through the body of the crystal, as water rushing through a jagged mountain stream. But as that energy is directed and abruptly focused through the petite termination, it is beamed out with a laser ray projection. This dual force of energetic motion enables the Laser Wands to be used for purposes that other crystals do not qualify for.

Before these crystals were transported onto the earth the angles were perfectly straight. But as they lowered their frequency to manifest on the physical plane, the denser vibrations of the material world shifted the angles as the crystals came into magnetic alignment with the poles of the earth. In doing so, the light traveling through the crystals became so intense that the shape of the angles was altered. Because of this, higher frequencies of light can be transmitted through these crystals that are alike in essence yet adjusted to the seemingly imperfect laws of the physical world.

USING LASER POWER

The laser beam of extremely intense light that is projected out of these crystal wands can be used to create energy force fields or protective shields around people or places. By holding the Laser Wand in your right hand and projecting a direct line of energy through the crystal, it is possible to define a force field that can be virtually impenetrable. To do so, draw right angles surrounding the object as you outline a square or rectangle shape around it. In other words, if you want to create a protective force field around your house or vehicle when you are going to leave it unattended, hold the termination away from the object as you walk around it, directing a beam through the crystal. If you want to surround people, children, or receivers of crystal healings with protection and light, project a laser ray through the wands as you walk around the person, defining the right angles that will seal their aura against negative influences. These crystals should not be pointed directly at people as they can cut through the auric field. Therefore, the crystal should be held with the termination pointing out and away from the person while defining the protective lines. This means that you would be inside the person's auric field, with your back towards them, directing the energy to the outside environment.

The Laser Wands have a special purpose in the art of invisibility. The energy beam that can be directed through these crystals when combined with the light from conscious human projection can be blindingly bright. Through dedicated use and advanced training, these crystals can create a force field surrounding you that will be like a barrier between your body, your aura, and the external world around you. The art of invisibility lies in the removal of attraction. You do not necessarily actually vanish. You instead project a strong light around you that other persons cannot see through, creating the illusion of disappearance. By increasing the force field until it merges with the frequency of existing light rays, you blend in with the surroundings and are unnoticed and unseen.

SURGICAL TOOLS

In advanced crystal healing practices, the Laser Wands can be used to perform such highly trained skills as psychic and emotional open heart surgery. These types of auric operations should only be done when the receiver is completely aware of the process and has already looked at, dealt with, and processed the attitudes, feelings, or attachments that the Laser Wand will cut away. Unless a person is truly ready and willing to release the thought patterns, concepts, and constricting emotional ties and identify with a more positive self-image the patterns will return to be further learned from. The healing that can occur with the use of these crystals is accomplished only when one is truly ready to let go of the earthly mire and align with a more refined sense of self. Generally several crystal healing sessions and a dedicated maintenance plan will precede any work done with the Laser Wands.

The laser beam of energy that is projected through these crystals is similar to that in which the psychic surgeons of the Philippines direct through their fingertips to separate the molecules of the flesh in order to enter into a dis-eased body. With the use of Laser Wands the intensity of light that is created when you, the healer, consciously project your own light through it can potentially cut through steel. But what is being cut through and removed are old ways of thinking, believing, and feeling that are not constructive to the individual's soul purpose.

The places most common to work with in this type of crystal healing are the chest and solar plexus areas where the emotional weeds choke the heart, or around the third eye or base of the neck (occiput) where old programming and mental patterns are stored.

Prior to using the Laser Wands in auric surgery, place Malachite on the solar plexus and Azurite on the third eye. These stones surface the mental (Azurite) and emotional (Malachite) patterns and the memories that are

Crystal Healing

responsible for creating them. Then, following the procedures in Part I, deal with it from the soul level. Coming to
understand the causes and purposes for such experiences,
realizing the evolution that has resulted, and learning the
lessons involved, it is then possible to sever the pattern
from the auric body through using Laser Wands.

The Laser Crystals become scalpels in your hands.
Using them is an incredible responsibility. You must be
very clearly guided before and while using them, and
should have prior training. In this way, Laser Wands are
like Black Obsidian (see *Crystal Enlightenment, Vol. I,*
page 93). You don't work with them on another person
without permission, and their understanding of the procedure and effects.

The scalpels are held with the thumb and middle
fingers on the sides of the crystal with the index finger on
the top. The ring finger and the pinkie can support the
crystal from the bottom or can be held out way from it.
The index finger is aligned with the planet Jupiter, which
emanates wisdom. As you direct your innate wisdom
through the Laser Wand, allow your hand to be guided
by the crystal as you cut the cords of attachment that bind
the soul in pain to the earth. The movement of the crystal
while in the act of cutting usually involves right angles,
again outlining a square or rectangle shape around the
area in which you are working. It is important to have
the receiver of the crystal healing breathe and consciously
focus light into the area as you cut away and draw out
the auric debris. The willing participation of your client
facilitates the complete removal of the old frequencies
and the healing process that follows the surgery.

Rose Quartz and Green Aventurine for the heart and
Gem Silica and Amethyst for the head are the main

LASER WAND

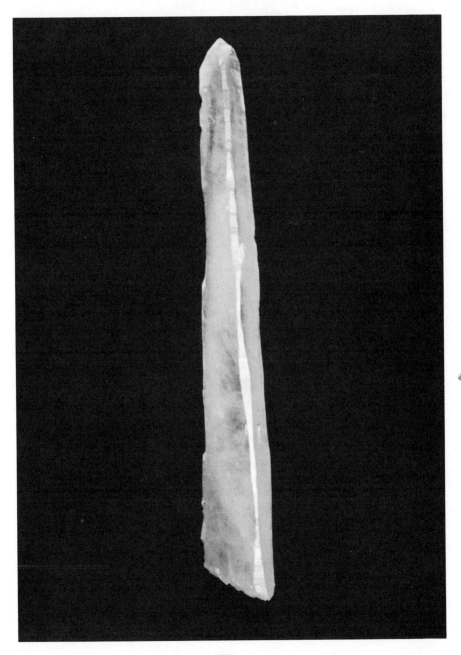

stones that are used after using Laser Wands. These stones usher in healing energy into the subjected areas so that trauma and disassociation do not occur. It is important to give extra healing energy following this type of practice. It is as if surgery had actually been done, and the Green Aventurine, Rose Quartz, Amethyst and Gem Silica are what stitches the area back together. In the days that follow the person receiving the healing should work with these stones as a part of their own personal maintenance plan.

Laser Wands can be used to help heal relationships by cutting the emotional cords of jealousy, insecurity, anger, sorrow or guilt. They can also be used to assist in breaking attachments towards people or things. In this case, discern from which chakra the attachment is emanating from. Then direct the Laser Wands over the area in three straight lines (one on top of the other) while your client breathes deeply and focuses the exhale on releasing and letting go. When attachment cords are cut an identity based in self love and personal security must be rebuilt. This is an essential responsibility in using these crystals in healing practices. The stones that work best for this are the heart chakra trinity—Rose Quartz, Kunzite, and Pink Tourmaline, as well as Green Aventurine.

Afterwards the receiver of the healing should be well grounded before driving a car or entering out into the busy world. Usually people are hypersensitive and feel a bit vulnerable following a Laser Wand session, and it would be best if they could take at least the rest of the day off to heal, process and integrate. It is a time when extra-special care should be given to oneself to insure complete healing and well being.

More than any other crystal, the Laser Wands require respect, attunement and guidance before using them in crystal healing practices and carry an incredible responsibility. As we learn from these specialized tools it will be possible to prevent many physical diseases from manifesting in the body by removing their mental and emotional counterparts beforehand.

CHAPTER XIII
THE EARTHKEEPERS

SURFACING GIANTS

The Earthkeeper Crystals are awesomely large quartz crystals that have only in the last year (1986) been located on the planet. These majestic specimens of light are being midwifed on to the surface of the earth by conscious miners and average five to seven feet in length and weigh seven to 8,500 pounds. These massive crystals are being mined from 30 to 60 feet underground and even in the heat of the day are ice cold to the touch. I was blessed to see several of these crystals when they arrived in the United States and hope to spend much more time around them. There are only a few Earthkeeper Crystals that have been mined to date. However, there is rumor of more.

The Earthkeepers are like giant redwood trees. Their auras grab your attention, baffling the mind with their enormous presence. They have weathered many earth-year rotations and in the process have embodied tremendous amounts of life experience. The Earthkeepers are a solid statement of life, growth, evolution, and perfection that cannot be ignored. Their presence warrants respect and their purpose is to take us beyond ourselves.

THE HISTORICAL LEGEND
OF THE
EARTHKEEPERS CRYSTALS

There is a very special story that surrounds the Earthkeeper Crystals, one of hope and inspiration. Sit back, relax, and I will share it with you.

A long, long time ago when the world was just a babe and the universe was younger, our earth was visited by advanced beings who originated much closer to the core of the galaxy and thrived on the abundant light source that emanated from the great central sun. Having more light available and being closer to the source of pure energy, they evolved at a rapid rate and took to the outer star systems in a quest for knowledge and adventure. As they gazed upon primal earth and witnessed the blue waters, the dense greenery, and the rich land, they named her Terra, meaning "the one who bears life."

Observing the natural physical laws governing Terra, they realized that she was ripe for conception. These beings, which we will refer to as The Elders, worked diligently with the elemental forces preparing the planet for the birth of conscious life forms. They used the natural earth stuff, silicon dioxide, and beamed into it their light force, creating huge Quartz crystals, known to us as the Earthkeepers. With the Earthkeeper Crystals as their predecessor, the electro-magnetic force field of the earth was set in preparation for their incarnation onto the physical plane. When the elements were right and the Earthkeeper Crystals had aligned the planet to a higher cosmic force, the Elders took human form and experienced the world of the senses. Many of them came and formed the root civilizations of Mu, Lemuria, and Atlantis, for they were the ancient ones which all myths, legends and religions refer to. They stood on the edge of time and were the master builders of universal evolution.

Also evolving on the planet at that time was Neanderthal man, who was an animal life form originating from the womb of Terra. The simultaneous existence of an animal breed and a highly evolved race of beings on the earth marked the beginning of a new cosmic cycle for Terra, one that could potentially lead her to her highest destiny.

The advanced civilizations used the Earthkeeper Crystals in their daily practices and bathed in their radiance. The crystals served to keep their consciousness attuned to the higher frequencies of their mother homeland, and all who came within their auric field were filled with power. They became powerful tools through which the cosmic force could be channeled to empower food, water, jewelry, and sacred robes which would then be worn. In certain cases these crystals were used as the judge in a court. Twelve people would stand around them, palm to palm, and when eight of the twelve received the same answer it was considered true.

As part of the divine plan for the advancement of the original species of the earth, it was decided that some of

EARTHKEEPER

the Elder souls would enter into the evolutionary cycle of the primates in order to eventually uplift them to the level of consciousness where they too would become attuned with the light force comprising the universe. Those who chose to stay and incarnate time and time again made a great sacrifice as they plunged into the world of matter, knowing that someday they would rise and with them take their fellow brothers and sisters. As this process occurred the memory veil was dropped and the remembrance of who they were and why they had come was hidden, so that they would become as one with the earthlings.

As time passed they became very accustomed to the earth and many became attached to the pleasures of the five senses and began to use the cosmic power generated from the crystals for their own personal fulfillment. They directed that force toward their own greed and purpose, which resulted in the eventual downfall of the root civilizations.

Seeing the dangerous misuse of power, many chose to leave Terra at that time and continue their work of evolutionary seeding. The ones who chose to stay eventually interbred with the earthlings and as a result of genetic mixing, a giant step in evolution was taken by the original inhabitants of earth. Thus, a new age of man was born. As the races merged a new breed of being was created and a new evolutionary cycle started, one that would take eons to complete. We are now on the threshold of that outcome, having become a refined race of beings capable of claiming the heritage of the stars from which the forefathers originated.

The Earthkeeper Crystals were buried deep within the earth at the time of the mass exodus from the planet. They were to be literally "the keepers of the earth" and

EARTHKEEPER

to watch over the progress and record the experience of the fall and rise of spirit into matter. When destiny manifested these giants once again onto the surface of the planet, they were to be the main device that would trigger the remembrance of the plan, lift the veils of forgotten memory, and reunite the consciousness of the ones who chose to stay with those who traveled on. The Earthkeepers, when activated by those who carry the ancient knowledge, will serve to embody the consciousness of the Elders, enabling the new race of Terra to establish consciousness communication with its celestial lineage. Once active, the Earthkeepers will also be able to transmit the knowledge of the evolution of life upon the earth to the Elders to be used for the development of consciousness on other worlds.

In many ways the Earthkeepers are like the symbolic monolith in that they arrived in ancient history and programmed (interbred) with the animal inhabitants and then were silent for thousands of years. When man was ready and had evolved to the point where he could reach out into the stars, the monolith[1] (the Earthkeepers) reappeared and directed their attention and focused their minds into realms of consciousness that they would have been unable to achieve on their own.

The Earthkeepers are here. They have come as great sages that carry within them not only the knowledge of the entire history of the earth, but also of life in the lighted stellar spaces from which their essence originated. They are manifestations of massive power and intelligence. They contain within them the wisdom of how to weather time, space, and physical plane existence, harvesting from it truth and love.

---

[1] Arthur C. Clarke, 2001, 2010, Space Odyssies

ACTIVATION

The Earthkeeper Crystals, when mined, are in an inactive state and have a thick milky frosting on their surface. The inside of the crystal is ice clear. It is as if the dusts of time need to be wiped off of them. When these crystals are activated, they will again serve to channel higher cosmic frequencies onto the planet, enabling accomplishment of conscious attunement and alignment with those forces.

Upon activation of these crystals we can learn the secrets of how to be in a physical body and in a material world, yet not be bound to it. When the Earthkeepers are in a state of complete activation their very presence will create greater awareness and expanded thinking. It would be of most benefit if these crystals were used in healing centers, communities, or group gatherings where many people could be exposed to their energies.

Their activation is dependent upon mergence with human thought forms. When twenty one people of like-mindedness gather around them in a circle, hold hands, and become of the same mind, the crystal will reawaken and the line of communication into the cosmic regions will be opened. The individuals forming the circle around the great Earthkeepers will unite their vibrational frequencies to become like the molecules in a crystal, in sync with cosmic energy. That willingness to let go of the personal ego sense of self and consciously merge into a greater whole is exactly the element needed to activate the Earthkeepers and link our collective consciousness to the knowledge, information, and energy that would otherwise be unattainable.

EVOKING GROUP CONSCIOUSNESS

When the Earthkeepers are worked with in group meditation practices they will assist individuals in expanding
their concept of "self" to include all the persons partici-
pating in the meditation. With unity of mind, oneness of
heart, and synchronicity of spirit, the power that a group
has to create positive change multiplies a thousandfold.
The Earthkeepers can teach us how to shift our one-track
focus and realize the multiple potentials that can be created when we learn to see beyond our noses and witness
the greater scheme of things. With all persons vibrating
at the same frequency around the great Earthkeepers, we
will be taught how to become "the keepers of the earth"
and a tremendous elevation for this planet will result. As
individuals learn to unite into groups in this way, the
unification of the human race into one being will be just
a step away. The impersonality that the Earthkeeper Crystals teach is not one of indifference, but rather of commit-
ted concern—to the degree of letting go of individual ego
interests in order to dedicate time, space, energy and
focus towards unity.

These crystals evoke positive action. They create harmony. They are here to unite us with the source from
which we sprang and to teach how to maintain our connection with both the earth and the heavens. These crystals carry within them the memory of being transported
here and can potentially teach us the art of time travel.
They can teach us how to maintain a physical existence
and also release our identity to it as we soar the higher
dimensions of reality. As a race we are ready. Ready again
to take a giant step in evolution and assist in aligning the
earth entity Terra to the cosmic rays emanating from the
great central sun at the core of the galaxy. When this

occurs human consciousness will totally reawaken to the realities that are now beyond comprehension. The Earth-keepers are part of that awakening and will inspire our latent potential and stimulate the dormant areas of our brains to embrace our ultimate destiny. Terra is becoming of age. She is ready to cross the threshold into maturity and adulthood and become one with the vast expanse of cosmic space of which she is a vital part.

PART III
MISCELLANEOUS TIDBITS

CHAPTER XIV
MISCELLANEOUS TIDBITS

The following chapters are dedicated to stones that I have gained an appreciation for since Volume I was printed, and other tidbits of information, reflections, and personal opinions.

RENEWING EVOLUTIONARY CONCEPTS

In the process of our social education we have been geared to see life in terms of an evolutionary hierarchy. In this type of mental programming we view the mineral world as the lowest form of life, then the plants, followed by the animals, and at the very top of the scale there we are, the mighty human! Well, I guess it depends on how you define "highest or most evolved." If we shift our thinking mode to say "that which is capable of living most in tune with the divine flow and reflecting the purest light is most evolved," then the human being often falls off of the throne.

Research into the plant kingdom proves that plants have feelings and definitely respond to love and kind vibrations. The dolphins are known to have a more advanced brain structure than humans and the instinctual tendencies of animals are often superior to the intellectual knowledge of man. The light reflected from crystals can often outshine the clouded auras of people who are emotionally and mentally stressed.

If we can open our minds to the fact that all forms of life are comprised of the same spirit and in reality none is greater or less than the other, then our love and appreciation of life will expand to include our oneness with it. As we receive all life as a part of ourselves, a vast world of knowledge will open up to us. Imagine sitting down with a rose and perceiving pure beauty, or swimming with the dolphins and having them share with you the knowledge that they have carried with them since the days of Atlantis. See yourself putting the termination of a Clear Quartz crystal to your brow and learning from it the secrets of light manifestation.

The art of interdimensional communication is possible on our own planet when we renew our evolutionary concepts to include all life on earth as being one and equal in spirit. Then and only then will true interdimensional communication with extra-terrestrial entities, celestial discarnates, and multi dimensional beings be possible. We all carry the same life force. We all equally claim the throne.

RECORD KEEPER APPEARANCE

In working closely with Record Keeper Crystals (see *Crystal Enlightenment, Vol. I*, page 65) I have personally witnessed amazing phenomenons take place. At times it is as if the records do not appear on the crystals until the person who is meant to have them is present to activate the sign of the triangular record into manifestation. On several occasions I have witnessed this to be so. When I get a new stock of crystals, I very carefully go through them and look for phantoms, rainbows, specific geometry, and Record Keepers. When the record appears in the exact moment that a specific person is present, then I know that crystal is meant to be used only by that particular individual. Record Keeper Crystals are most often neatly tucked away into my private collection when they reveal themselves to me. Yet I am finding that some Record Keepers obviously wait to present their true identity and purpose in the presence of their co-worker in order to be worked with by that special person.

On one occasion I was giving a lecture at a very established non-metaphysical place and had no intentions of getting into such "out there" information as Record Keeper Crystals. As I was ready to pass around a large Generator Crystal for the people to look at (that I had previously passed around two other workshops and knew very well), dozens of records appeared on it before my eyes. In amazement I stopped in the middle of a sentence and said, "Oh my God, this is a major Record Keeper!" To which the class innocently responded, "What is a Record Keeper?" As I explained the story of the Record Keepers to them, I said to myself, "This crystal is obviously for someone here." Sure enough, a woman in the group could not let go of it and knew beyond the shadow of a doubt that she needed to work with that crystal. This type of experience has happened several times in my practice.

So, keep your eyes open and don't be surprised if one day when you least expect it, triangles appear before your eyes as the crystal shines one of its faces and says, "Guess what! We have work to do!"

DEMATERIALIZATION

There are many accounts of crystals that have completely disappeared from sight for no apparent reason. No amount of search can recover them, for they have dematerialized from the physical plane in order to do their work in the subtle bodies. It is as if these crystals implant themselves in your aura in order to facilitate a clearing, a healing, a balancing, or to assist in attracting certain forces into your life. Sometimes these vanishing artists will reappear in material form—oftentimes in the exact same place that you knew you left them or where you have looked for them a dozen times. Other times it is not necessary for them to rematerialize as they have become permanently implanted in the auric field. If so, don't mourn. They have moved on to a higher frequency and are still serving you by increasing the light force around your body. In the dematerialized state the crystal can actually assist in clearing the mental and emotional bodies and sealing auric holes that can make one vulnerable to negative influences. The conscious attunement to crystals that have dematerialized can serve to open your mind to the unmanifest realities that exist beyond the normal scope of sensual vision. With the light forces of dematerialized crystals at work in your energy field, the process of personally learning the art of dematerialization is facilitated if you choose to consciously focus on that phenomenon.

MAN-MADE AND POLISHED CRYSTALS

There are many man cut (artificially formed) and polished Quartz crystals flooding the market today. Personally I have never been attracted to such crystals and on certain occasions have even been repelled by them. After much deliberation I now understand the reason why.

Quartz crystals in and of themselves exist in a natural state of perfected form. They vibrate at a level of cosmic harmony because each individual component is aligned to the cosmic force. In other words, the electrons and protons that comprise the atoms, the atoms that create the molecules, and the molecular lattice forming the building blocks for the mineral are all vibrating at the same frequency. (There is no random ordering.) In doing so they are innately aligned with the primal creative force and manifest in true form a radiant expression of cosmic harmony and material perfection. That is why you can just hold or wear a Quartz crystal and it will seek to also align your vibration with its own unified essence.

Unless a lapidary artist is very skilled, trained, and attuned to the frequency of a crystal, attempts to alter its natural form often fall short of manifesting the true reflection of the atomical and molecular particles that are innately attuned to cosmic frequency. I have seen crystals that have been so traumatized through the meager human attempt to improve upon them that nothing I could do could neutralize the effects. I have seen naturally single terminated generators turned into double terminated crystals by faceting the opposing end, and terminated crystals created when it was obvious that no termination existed. I have even seen five faces on a Quartz crystal instead of six, and at one time someone tried to sell me a cut crystal as a natural one that upon examination had seven cut faces forming the termination. The edges on these crystals are often softened and dull and are less effective in channeling healing energy than naturally formed crystals. I also know that a lot of this type of work is now being done in third world countries where labor is very cheap and the technology in the delicate art of cutting crystals is very low.

It is not that to polish or cut a crystal is not good or ethical, it is just that to do so one must be very in tune with the nature of the crystal in order to do it justice. To polish the face of a crystal to bring out its natural beauty or to repair a chip in a termination often lends great assistance to the beauty, purpose and value of a stone. What I am opposed to is the complete alteration of the already perfected natural form.

On the other hand, these crystals are often cut from large pieces of unterminated material that otherwise might be crushed for technological purposes and fashioning them in this way can potentially raise their vibration and allow them to serve in a higher capacity. I have also met people who were very consciously and lovingly cutting crystals for use in healing and have talked with some folks who work extensively with cut crystals with positive results. The bottom line is, don't take my word for it.

Check it out for yourself and experiment. Find one of each kind, place them alternately to your heart and third eye, and see what they relay to you.

MORE CLEANSING
AND RECHARGING TECHNIQUES

For centuries the American Indians have used sacred herbs for cleansing and purification. Cedar and sage are the most powerful aromatic healing herbs in this tradition, and can also be used to cleanse crystals. By lighting these herbs and allowing the fragrant smoke to surround crystals and healing stones, they are purified in a most delightful way. Before and after each crystal healing I have set up the practice to light smudge sticks (combination of cedar and sage), not only to cleanse the crystals but also to clear the air of any residue from the healing that may be lurking in the ethers. This wonderul aroma can also be used in various purification practices. i.e., before meditation, in sweat lodges or saunas, to cleanse the environment after arguments or conflicts, or before moving into a new space to clear away the old energies.

Another way to recharge crystals and stones is by placing them under a pyramid structure. All of my wands, scalpels and frequently used generators have taken up permanent residence inside pyramids. The perfected geometric structure of the pyramid lends its cosmic energies to purify and energize whatever is contained within them. Placing traumatized, radiated, or overused crystals inside of pyramids over extended periods of time is one of the only ways that I have found to restore them to proper balance.

CHOOSING SINGLE GENERATORS FOR PERSONAL HEALING PRACTICES

There are several things to look for when in the market for a Single Generator to use in a healing practice. One of the most important factors to be aware of is the termination. It is best if there are no chips or nicks in the point or the faces comprising the termination. Also in observing the faces of the termination, it is of most benefit if at least one of the facets is a perfect triangle. This will allow for energy to move in a direct beam as it travels from the bottom of the crystal through the base of the triangular face, along opposing symmetrical sides, and out of the termination. Also, the clearer the inside of the crystal the better. The inner clarity is important in enabling your own healing energy to be purely transmitted through the crystal.

The generators that you use in your healing practice (or for your personal meditations) become charged with your own vital force. As you beam your healing light through Single Generators, your energy is being purified, magnified and intensified as it passes through the crystal and is beamed out of the termination. These personal crystal friends and partners in healing you may not want to have anyone else touch so that their alignment with you is undisturbed. Having these crystals charged with your own healing force, they also come in handy when you are personally feeling off-centered, imbalanced, or in need of healing energy.

THE RAINBOW RAY

The Rainbow Ray has a very beautiful lesson to share with us. In our skies rainbows are created when sunlight reflects off of miniature water crystals and prismatically transforms them into an arc of color that reaches down from the heavens to kiss the earth. The very nature of the elements necessary to create such a spectacular event can be related to symbolically. The sun is the light that is often blocked from the heavy rain clouds of life, but when the light breaks through, when the spirit beams forth, one of the most beautiful sights is witnessed when out of the dark and damp comes a spectacular array of colors proving that all is in perfect order. It is of most benefit to be outside and breathe deeply whenever a rainbow is in the sky to absorb the colorful healing rays, even if it means getting a little wet!

The rainbow teaches us not to look at just any one aspect of anything. It shows us how to look at the many different rays of life; at the joy, at the anger, the sadness and the beauty all at once. Rainbows contain it all in balance and perfection. The pink is the joy, the green the healing, and the blue beams forth the peace.

Rainbows are also often found in Quartz crystals. Surprisingly enough, they are usually born inside of crystals that have been included from perhaps a fall or some trauma when growing within the womb of the earth. Again the rainbow teaches us that it is through the hard knocks that we learn to balance the many faces of life as the impenetrable light shines through the dark times.

Rainbows are a symbol of hope and inspiration that when embodied in quartz (or other crystals) represent the ability to make the very best out of life, and in so doing the prismatic ladder of light into the heavens can be climbed. Rainbows are a direct link from the earth into the ethers through which prayers, hopes, dreams and visions can traverse. Rainbow crystals are therefore very beneficial to work with when praying or sending healing energy out to other people.

The rainbow is a symbol of unity as it blends each color harmoniously with the rest, demonstrating for us how to embrace the elements in our life. The rainbow proves that it is indeed possible to bridge one energy to another, one chakra to the next. Rainbow Crystals are very powerful to work with in personal meditations when consciously concentrating on connecting energy centers. When a crystal containing a rainbow within it is placed between two energy centers that are not integrated, it will serve to bind them together in unison. In this way Rainbow Crystals can be used to unify the chakra system in crystal healing or can be personally meditated with, carried or worn when one is in the process of learning the lessons of the rainbow ray. By consciously attuning to Rainbow Crystals, they will transmit into the aura the ability to view things with a not-so-serious attitude and demonstrate how to live with joy and humor in all that we do.

EMPATHETIC CRYSTALS

At times it may be difficult to imagine that a crystal or stone actually knows what you are thinking or feeling. They do not have nervous systems, so how can they feel? They do not have a brain, so how can they think? They do not behave as we humans behave, so how can they have any sense of what it is like for us? Well, it's true. Crystals and stones are a very different type of life form than we are and their dimension of reality is certainly not the same, but who is to say that in their own magnificent unknown way that they cannot be sensitive to what we are all about. In my experience in the crystal world, I have witnessed many occasions where crystals and stones not only felt what was going on, but responded in a loving, supportive, and even sometimes sacrificial way.

A good friend of mine was working very closely with the Rose Quartz cabachon stone in her meditations every day while she was consciously focusing on loving herself more. In the process many unresolved inner conflicts were arising. One day after a meditation in which she had been clutching the stone tightly while releasing an old emotional charge, she placed the stone on her altar, stood up, and was about ready to leave the room when the stone burst into a dozen pieces. As it did, she felt an immediate release of emotional pressure and knew that she had been healed. She bent down to pick up the pieces of the stone that she had loved so much, and realized that the Rose Quartz had not only felt her pain but had taken on the emotional burden and in the process of releasing it had actually sacrificed itself.

This is not an uncommon story for Rose Quartz, being the love stone, the healer of emotional wounds, and the cornerstone for the heart chakra, teaching self love and forgiveness. For this very reason it is important to cleanse Rose Quartz often when using it in healing practices. It is one of the New Age Stones and can take on the sorrows of humans, often unto its death. Often when Rose Quartz has been hard at work on our heart chakras the stone will turn cloudy and dull, losing its natural luster. This should be taken as a direct sign to cleanse the stone and allow it to regenerate so that it can do its work without giving its life.

Single Quartz generator crystals have been known to crack during crystal healings when auric work was being done with them and major transitions were occurring. Jewelry has been noticeably dulled or has even shattered when worn on particularly stressful days, and crystals and stones become less lustrous if neglected or misused. On the other hand, personal meditation crystals can become clear when once clouded as we send our love and good thoughts into them, and healing stones become even more powerful when they are used consciously, cared for, and appreciated. It is the responsibility of the people who are working with crystals and stones to cleanse them regularly and give back to them the elements they need for survival; mainly water, sunlight, attention, and love.

SELF-HEALED CRYSTALS

Most of the time a crystal will terminate at one end. On special occasion they will double terminate. Equalling the speciality of a double terminated crystal is one that has naturally terminated at the base. These types of crystals do not come to a six sided terminated peak or apex, as double terminated crystals do, but they are naturally formed instead of looking broken on the opposing end.

Crystals usually grow out from a hard rock surface which serves as a base from which one end of the crystal is able to protrude. Double terminated crystals form in much softer clay and have no hard rock limitations, and therefore can grow from both ends and form double apexes. In naturally terminated crystals one end has been broken or separated from the hard rock foundation at some point in its development, and then continued to terminate at the base even though it did not have the space or the environment to form a completed apex termination. These are called self-healed crystals, for even though they were separated from their secure base they still continued to reach a natural state of perfection and formed smaller yet no less special terminated faces.

Self-healed crystals are easy to find if you look at the base of a single Quartz generator crystal and observe the markings. If the crystal has an unfinished bottom and looks rocklike, then it is not self-healed and naturally terminated. But, if upon observance you witness a beautifully laced design of finished edges, you know that you have found a master in the art of self-healing.

Self-healed crystals have learned in their evolutionary process how to mend and heal themselves and can therefore lend their knowledge and share their experience in teaching us a similar lesson. These crystals can become great companions during our own self-healing process, or they can make wonderful partners and assistants in crystal healing practice. You can place self-healed crystals in the hands of the recipient of a crystal healing or over any area to relay to the body, the psyche, the heart, or the subconscious the art of healing the self. These crystals know how to take situations that appear to be devastating and make the very best out of them, finding perfect order and natural completion.

STRIATED POWER
FEATURING
TOURMALINE, GOLDEN TOPAZ, KUNZITE AND AQUAMARINE

There are several crystal formations that display parallel striations running the length of the crystal. Tourmaline, Kunzite, Topaz and Aquamarine are all apparent in this natural phenomenon. Whenever these lines of energy are made manifest, it indicates that the dynamic power accompanied with a high electrical charge will rapidly travel through the body of the crystal. The striations are like electrical wires through which a high voltage current can be transmitted into the physical plane.

Each of the above crystals terminate, which sets the direction in which the energy will move. For example, if a naturally terminated Pink Tourmaline was placed above the heart chakra pointing towards the throat, it would channel the expression of love through the voice and into the power of the spoken word. Pointing the termination of a Topaz crystal into the navel will direct the golden ray of the crown into the physical body for manifestation of the conscious will.

Pink Kunzite is the activator of the heart chakra and its force dynamically transforms insecurities and inhibitions into loving action. Tourmaline, in its variety of colors, heals and strengthens the bodily systems, enabling the spirit force to infiltrate into the nervous system. Aquamarine will stimulate an increased functioning of the throat chakra, facilitating the higher octave of the voice to be utilized in the expression of truth. Depending upon the direction the termination is pointed, Golden Topaz crystals will either transmit energy of the crown into the body or direct the physical appetites towards the consciousness centers.

Keep your eyes out for these and other crystals that will possess the geometric design of long striated lines protruding in parallel perfection. It will mean power and the ability to channel a dynamic force into whatever area they are worked with. These striated stones, more than any other crystalline formation, will transmit high frequency energy onto the material plane and into the body for activation of the chakras and strengthening of the physical systems for spiritual transformation.

THE MENTAL TRINITY:
FLUORITE, CALCITE AND PYRITE

I would like to introduce to you three stones that I have come to love, respect and use often when working with the mind and associated mental development. They are Fluorite, Calcite and Pyrite. Interestingly enough these stones are frequently mined in the same vicinity and often even grow side by side or on top of one another. Pyrite is often found in Fluorite octahedrons or growing with Flourite clusters. Calcite is also commonly found with its good friend Fluorite. They all have a great deal in common and serve a similar function and purpose in affecting and stabilizing the frequencies of the higher mind.

Fluorite is for channeling the intuitive power of the mind into physical activity. Calcite is the stone to use when mental transitions, adjustments and alterations are taking place. Pyrite strengthens mental capacity and develops the higher faculties of the human mind. Pyrite facilitates the growth of higher knowing, Calcite assists in easing out the old attitudes and concepts so greater knowledge can occur, and Fluorite will put that higher knowledge into action on the physical plane.

This mental trinity is a great combination of stones to work with when studying, when working on changing old mental patterns or when consciously developing the psychic abilities. These stones are wonderful helpers for channels, psychics or professional counselors.

During crystal healing layouts, Fluorite, Pyrite or Calcite can be placed at the third eye center to stimulate higher brain wave frequencies or placed at the base of the skull to reawaken latent intelligence. They can be worn, meditated with or used for their assistance in integrating the intellect with the intuition and in the development of the IQ.

THE NAVEL CONNECTION: GOLDEN TOPAZ AND RUTILATED QUARTZ

The navel center is where our personal power becomes manifest onto the physical plane. Its color is orange yellow and its energy is vital to our happiness and fulfillment. If the navel center is constricted or blocked the ability to project our conscious will into the workings of our daily lives is drastically limited. The navel center forms the apex of the lower triangle of energy which includes the first, second and third chakras and governs our physical plane action and sense of personal identity.

Similar in color frequency to the navel is the golden ray which resides at the crown chakra and empowers an individual with personal identification of the infinite spirit. Being similar in color vibration to the yellow of the navel center, the crown chakra can have a direct influence over the government of will through the body. With the crown chakra directly connected to the navel the possibilities of manifesting divine power onto the earth are increased a thousandfold.

Miscellaneous Tidbits

There are three main stones that can be used at the navel center to channel the crown's golden wisdom into daily action. These are Citrine (featured in *Crystal Enlightenment, Vol. I*, page 86), Rutilated Quartz and Golden Topaz. Each of these stones has the power to transmute negative habit patterns and habitual tendencies into conscious action governed by the empowered will.

Naturally terminated Golden Topaz crystals when placed with the apex pointing directly at the navel center will channel the crown chakra's intention into the body's power station. If you, on the other hand, want to focus excess physical plane power towards the energy centers of consciousness in the head, the termination would be pointing up towards the heart. This is usually done when a person is too self centered, consumed with business, or manifesting workaholic tendencies. Being striated (see Striated Power, page 179), Golden Topaz will channel high frequency electrical currents through the body of the crystal, bringing strength and increased energy into any area in which they are placed.

Rutilated Quartz is clear or smokey with small golden rutile needles running through it. These golden lines of energy become super charged by quartz's innate dynamic presence and in so doing become channels through which the golden energy of the crown can dive into the roots of the earth. Naturally terminated Rutilated Quartz generators can be used in the same manner as Golden Topaz crystals. Cut, polished, faceted, or cabachon stones of Rutilated Quartz can be used in crystal healing layouts on or around the navel center to activate will power. They can also be placed around any area in need of extra energy and are often used in conjunction with Malachite at the solar plexus to assist in dissipating excess emotional charge.

Golden Topaz, Rutilated Quartz and Citrine can also be used at the crown chakra when one wants to gain greater perspective and insight into the soul's connection with the infinite and the purpose of existence.

CHAPTER XV
MORE HEALING STONES

GEM STONES

A gem stone could be any one of a dozen different stones. "Gem stone" is a collective name for any stone that possesses a precious quality, with high transparency and has no (or relatively few) flaws in the inner makeup. The most common gemstones are: Diamonds, Rubies, Sapphires, and Emeralds. However, any crystalline formation can manifest its gem quality specimens.

One of the characteristics of a gem stone is that it is hard enough to be cut, faceted and polished with man-made skill and labor. With the help of human technology, gemstones become worth a fortune to those who love to adorn themselves with riches. Gem stones have an enduring beauty unsurpassed by semi-precious stones or mineral specimens and to a large degree the credit has to go to the lapidary artist who takes rough, uncut, often unattractive material and transforms it into brilliant jewels.

Crystal Healing

Gem stones are usually small and sell by the carat. Prices vary depending on the weight and quality of the stone. Because of the size and price of gem stones, they are not always included in the collection of healing stones. However, they can be of great value in crystal healing. Because the light reflected off of gem stones will bounce off of each faceted face, the stone will reflect a very clear ray of color back into the aura. For example, if a deep indigo Sapphire was placed at the third eye, it would enable one to accomplish the same penetrating effect as if you had used several Azurite nodules. Rubies at the second energy center can stimulate the sexual appetite or activate the creative forces to be channeled to other energy centers as no other red stone can do. The brilliant green radiance of Emeralds will transmit negative energies into rays of powerful healing force and the Diamond is the only stone that outdoes Clear Quartz in clarity and brilliance at the crown.

One of the best ways to use gem stones is in remedies (see *Crystal Enlightenment, Vol. I*, page 18). In this way it is possible to take full advantage of the high frequency power of gem stones without having to invest a fortune in the process.

Gem quality Amethyst, Citrine, Topaz, Tourmaline and many other stones demonstrate the ability to express clarity, transparency, beauty and radiance and can be classified as gem stones. Whenever you work with gem stones you are working with a very clear light force and a high degree of reflective power. For that reason gem stones have always been held in high esteem and in ancient days their forces were consciously used in the formation of jewelry, crowns and ornamentation. Besides their physical beauty and their intrinsic value, these gem quality specimens are also bearers of very clear, powerful light rays capable of channeling their forces for our upliftment.

INDICOLITE—
BLUE TOURMALINE

Indicolite transmits the blue ray of peace more powerfully than any other stone on the planet. Being in the Tourmaline family (see *Crystal Enlightenment, Vol. I*, page 126), Indicolite carries a high electrical charge as it channels currents of positive energy along its long parallel striations. If Tourmaline is rubbed briskly a natural heat is created and the electrical charge of the stone can be felt as one end becomes positive (the termination) while the opposite becomes negative (the base). This natural heat can be directed through the crystal into any area where peaceful energy is needed, i.e., homes, offices, children's rooms, hearts, etc.

The Tourmaline family has a large variety of colors through which to manifest. Indicolite claims the blue spectrum, ranging from the lightest clearest pale shades of blue into the depths of indigo. Long slender powerful Indicolite wands can be found displaying the full ray of hue from dark deep blue at the base through azure to terminate at a peak of clear ice blue. These magic wands are very special. Through them the courageous strength of peace can be channeled onto the earth. These wands are a gift and will find their way to those who are willing to be at peace in their own lives and consciously use the power of the wands to bring that state of tranquility into the world. Indicolite wands can be used as generators in the aura during crystal healings to assist in dissolving mental friction or emotional constriction.

Blue Tourmaline stones can be used in crystal healing layouts in any area in need of a dynamic peaceful ray. They are especially good to place over the third eye area to ease a troubled mind or at the heart center to calm an angry or saddened heart. Since blue is the color for the throat chakra, Indicolite is a perfect stone to place at the throat center to enable clear verbal expression. It is also a stone that can be used for the higher expressions of sound through the voice and is frequently used by singers, lecturers and channels. Since necklaces are worn around the neck and close to the throat chakra point, Blue Tourmaline can be easily worn to continually activate the powers of verbal expression through the throat center. It is one of the best stones to wear for chronic sore throats, thyroid problems, speech impediments and other related throat chakra ailments as it channels healing peace while simultaneously energizing and strengthening.

GARNET

Ranging in color from emerald green to orange and into the deepest reds, Lady Garnet expresses herself beautifully in a variety of hues. Garnets are usually small and beautifully faceted stones and are fairly inexpensive to acquire. They are usually seen in jewelry. However, they can be effectively used in crystal healing layouts.

The color range covered by this stone affects the areas from the heart into the second chakra. This area can become constricted if the creative vitality of the second (sexual) center is unable to circulate due to emotional tension at the solar plexus. When this occurs creative energy is usurped and one feels lethargic, uninspired, or suicidal. In these cases Green Garnet can be used in conjunction with Red Garnet at the solar plexus to channel healing energy and vital force for the proper assimilation and integration of creativity through the emotional centers.

Red Garnets are the most common and demonstrate the pure energetic power of red. They are particularly good to use at the second chakra during crystal healing layouts to initiate rejuvenation, creativity, regeneration and blood purification. They can also be used over any other chakra points to stimulate the creative expression of that particular energy center. For example, when Red Garnets are used with Amethyst at the third eye center the creative power of the intuitive forces are activated.

When worn or meditated with, Garnets will increase creative energy and can activate the sexual appetite. Therefore, these stones are very good to use for people who are unable to sexually express themselves. Garnets have been known to be of value in cases of infertility, sterility and frigidity. Through continued use with these stones, one could learn how to directly channel the creative force of the second chakra to any of the other energy centers for a multitude of expressive experiences.

GREEN AVENTURINE

Green Aventurine is quartz that reflects a true, pure green ray. It often has little sparkles in it that bring dazzle and joy to the stone. Green Aventurine is one of the best stones to use in crystal healing layouts when you want to soothe a troubled heart, neutralize the emotions, and bring a sense of balance and well being into the physical body.

Essentially Green Aventurine can be used for any ailment, whether mental, emotional or physical. Its pure green healing essence can penetrate through any problem and lend its vibration to comfort any aspect of being. Being quartz, it has a very high dynamic charge that empowers it to dissolve unhealthy thoughts, feelings and related physical problems. Green Aventurine can be placed on top of any part of the body that is dis-eased or imbalanced to reflect the green healing ray into the aura, as well as to penetrate its essence directly into the physical body. Green Aventurine stones can be carried or worn during times of stress and turmoil to assist in keeping a person balanced and harmonized within. If one stone could be named as an all-around healer, it would be Green Aventurine, known for its dynamic power to soothe, heal and balance.

In crystal healing layouts it is especially good to use around the heart chakra and solar plexus areas to assist in neutralizing suppressed emotions. Its purpose is not to surface or mirror emotions such as Malachite, but more to dissolve whatever feelings are creating heart or solar plexus constriction. Therefore, it is a good stone to use in conjunction with Malachite when you are consciously working to clear emotional congestion from the solar plexus area. Malachite will surface and Green Aventurine will soothe. Green Aventurine is also a true friend to Rose Quartz, working together to heal and align the heart chakra.

GREEN CALCITE, GOLD CALCITE

Calcite in general is a mental stone. Green Calcite is specifically a mental healer and can be used in any situation when one is striving to reach mental balance. Green

More Healing Stones

Calcite softens the often rigid boundaries of the intellectual mind so that true inner knowing can come into play. It is especially good for children who are having a hard time intellectualizing in school room discussions. It is also ideal for people with mental disorders or for use when consciously trying to reprogram old attitudes and thought patterns.

Often in the process of healing ourselves it is necessary to readjust our thoughts to encompass a greater reality. Green Calcite can be there in those times to assist immensely in the release of old outdated concepts and the acknowledgments of new ones. There is often an attachment and a security that is placed around what is known, even if it is not what is true. Green Calcite lends its healing green force to ease the old out and usher the new in. It is as if it can be there to say to the old reality forms, "It's okay, you can become a part of a much greater whole if you surrender." And it is as if the mind listens when Green Calcite speaks. Green Calcite talks the language of the intellect in a way that is so non-offensive as to be completely trusted.

This stone is good to use at the third eye center or at the base of the neck during crystal healing layouts when consciously working on releasing old mental patterns. It is also good to use around the heart chakra to communicate to the emotions that are often associated with thought patterns that to let go is to surrender to a higher and greater force. Green Calcite is a good stone to carry or wear when mental changes are occurring. It is a healer and a friend in times of transition and readjustment.

When mental or emotional patterns become very rigid and set, one of the places that they will manifest in

dis-ease in the physical body is in the bones and associated ligaments, cartilage and tendons. Green Calcite is
therefore a very good stone to use in cases of arthritis,
tendonitis, rheumatism or any osteopathic problem. This
stone can also be used in any sports injuries or accidents
involving bone ligament damage. Green calcite is a great
partner to chiropractors and osteopaths in assisting them
to channel healing energy directly into bone tissue.

Because of the cooling light green shade Green Calcite reflects, it can also be used in any situation where an
excess of red energy is creating imbalance. Fevers can be
cooled, burns healed and anger-related symptoms eased
by using this stone. By placing a Green Calcite stone on
the body next to the area of distress while mentally and
visually concentrating healing energy into the area on the
inhale and releasing the stress, pain and constriction on
the exhale, miraculous healings can occur. It is important
to apply this practice for 15 minutes at least four times a
day to insure success and long lasting effects. It is also
important to cleanse the stone after each session and
leave it to recharge on a clear quartz cluster or inside a
pyramid structure (see *Crystal Enlightenment*, Cleansing
Stones, pages 26–27).

A partner worth mentioning in the same family as
Green Calcite is Gold Calcite. Still maintaining the mental quality, Gold Calcite has the power to channel the
highest mental faculties of the crown chakra into the physical body for manifestation if placed at the navel center
during crystal healing layouts. It can also be used at the
crown chakra to stimulate the higher frequencies of
thought power to be projected into creative endeavors.
Gold Calcite is a good stone to meditate with, wear, or
carry when you need to be mentally alert and sharp with
the powers of the higher mind.

TIGER'S EYE

Tiger's Eye is one of the most unique and fascinating stones in the quartz family, ranging in color from light to dark brown with golden yellow highlights. Being a member of the quartz family, Tiger's Eye innately carries a high vibrational charge, yet the depth of the dark brown ray grounds that energy into the roots of the earth.

Tiger's Eye has two distinct energies present. The depth of the brown background is the very richness of the earth which has been delicately laced with the golden ray of the crown chakra. This combination of energies enables Tiger's Eye to be used at the navel center to ground the elevated consciousness of the crown into physical reality. When Tiger's Eye is placed on the navel center during crystal healing layouts, one can notice a direct influx of higher energies entering into the body, creating an overall sense of well being.

The silky gold sheen that reflects the eye of the tiger symbolizes personal power, integrity and the ability to bring heaven to earth. The eye of the tiger can see through the illusionary limitations of physical plane laws and into it infuse the miraculous glory of the spirit. Tiger's Eye can give one the power to see God in all material forms while simultaneously serving to develop will power.

This is a stone that I have gained much respect and appreciation for and I think you will too. Tiger's Eye rates as one of the main navel chakra stones equal in prestige to Citrine and Golden Topaz, yet more grounding. This is a particularly good stone to use with people who are spaced out, uncommited to life, or unable to manifest their will through action.

HAWK'S EYE

A very good friend and Quartz comrade to Tiger's Eye is Hawk's Eye (sometimes referred to as Falcon's Eye). Tiger's Eye manifests a yellow-gold sheen, whereas in Hawk's Eye blue gray to blue green is contrasted against a deep black brown. These stones are fascinating to look at in the sunlight as the fractures and silky lustre shifts angles as they are rotated. This iridescent quality makes Hawk's Eye popular stones to be used in jewelry and ornamentation.

Hawk's Eye is one of the emerging power stones for the base chakra. This stone will greatly assist one to gain proper perspective on issues or situations in daily life. If placed at the first chakra point in crystal healing layouts (see *Crystal Enlightenment*, Chakra Points Chart, page 165), worn, or meditated with, Hawk's Eye will bring a deep peace and healing into the physical realities. It is one of the best stones to use in cases where you are working with negative patterns that are manifesting into physical dis-ease, as it brings a peaceful healing ray directly into the body.

Representing the eye of the hawk, this stone symbolizes the ability to see earth and all physical occurrences as if you were gazing down upon it from above. Hawks have always been associated as the messengers of the gods to the people. This stone can assist in giving insight into the workings of third dimensional existence and can facilitate understanding of how the world works, better enabling one to consciously work with the laws of the earth to manifest personal goals. Hawk's Eye are known for the ability to empower the human mind with the vision necessary to see life with a much broader perspective and can be placed upon the third eye for such purposes. One of the most pleasurable of the dark stones, Hawk's Eye lends grounding qualities in a manner easily submitted to. Working together as a duo, Hawk's Eye and Tiger's Eye can assist in creating a dynamic experience of heaven on earth.

HERKIMER DIAMONDS

What bright beams of sunlight! What absolutely brilliant specimens of angle and radiance. Herkimer Diamonds reflect light off their many apexing faces and take the first prize at the show for natural terminations. Herkimer Diamonds are quartz crystals that are mined only in Herkimer, New York. They often look like double terminated Quartz and indeed they are double and sometimes triple and quadruplely terminated. Herkimer Diamonds often have small herkies growing off the sides of them and very rarely display an unterminated face. Their multiterminated factor is what gives them that extra charge of dynamic power.

Herkimer Diamonds are one of the best stones to use in crystal healing layouts to clear and dissolve an emotionally tense or congested area. When placed between chakras they will serve to clear the passageways for clear energy to flow between two centers. That is why Herkimer Diamonds work very well with Malachite at the solar plexus area. Malachite will surface suppressed emotions and the diamonds of quartz will dissolve and dissipate it.

Herkimer Diamonds are great to carry with you when you feel you need that little extra boost of energy.

They are often beautifully set in jewelry and can make any area in which they are placed become dazzling. They have been known to be of value when placed under the pillow during sleep states to initiate conscious out of the body experiences or to enable accurate recollection of dream activity. Herkimer Diamonds are indeed a delight. They are happy. They will help keep you happy too!

OPAL

Opal is a very mysterious and fascinating stone displaying a rainbow-like iridescence changing the play of colors with the angle of observance. This opalescent reflection phenomenon is one of the factors responsible for Madam Opal's elusive nature. Varying depths of color will appear when viewed from different angles as she never really stabilizes her personality enough to be directly encountered. Ms. Opal can only be appreciated for her ever-changing light shows and color effects as she plays upon the pleasure of your senses.

Opals always contain water which will act upon the emotional body when worn or meditated with. This is a stone that can be successfully worked with only by those who are emotionally balanced. Otherwise Opal will magnify and intensify whatever emotional state is prevailing. This unique stone reflects the human emotional body and in so doing mirrors it back at you in an intensified state. If a person is angry or upset, Opal will increase the negative force of red energy. If on the other hand a person is depressed and insecure, it will add depth to the feeling. If, however, a person is secure, balanced and at peace within, Opal will shine every facet of their radiant being.

Because Opal contains up to thirty percent water, one must be sensitive in the care of these stones. If they are cracked they could lose their water, which is responsible for the opalescence. The aging process is avoided and opalescence increased if the stones are kept in moist absorbent cotton or on a Quartz cluster. They should not be stored near the heat, as this could evaporate their vital water source. Without that water, without her fiery emotion, Madam Opal loses her dynamic color and her very life force.

Opals are actually a distant member of the Quartz family and are divided into three main groups: the Opalescent Precious Opals, the Fire Opals, and the Common Opals. Precious Opals are usually white or milky with a color array matrix included within. Precious quality is also found in dark blue, dark green, dark grays, and on rare occasion found in black. Fire Opals are named after their orange color and are usually milky and dense, rarely displaying opalescence. Fire Opals should not be worn by those people who are known to have suppressed anger or who are potentially volatile as Opal will intensify that energy. Common Opals are mostly opaque and without dynamic plays of color and can be found ranging from clear transparent to yellow brown.

Opals are not usually used in crystal healing layouts unless a person wants to intensify the emotional state. They are most successfully used by those who are aware of the effects and have the understanding that as emotional changes occur, Opal will empower each emotion. Madam Opal is very sensitive to our stresses and is as moody as we can be. But, when we stabilize our emotional body, Opal's water will clearly reflect the heart's loving light. Opals can therefore be consciously worn or used when joyous and exuberant feelings wish to be magnified. Ms. Opal will be a friend if you will be a friend to yourself.

CHAPTER XVI
DON'T TAKE IT SO SIRIUS!

PERSPECTIVES

Each individual has a unique perspective on life and what it is all about. Personal views stem from our experiences that have subsequently led to beliefs and concepts about life. To a large degree our personal reality has also been dictated and programmed into our thinking from society, institutions, religions, and formal parental thinking modes that we were exposed to during the formative years. Life and reality as we have conceived it to be may or may not be true and serving our greatest potential. So often we get stuck in a mind-set of thoughts, attitudes, and beliefs that actually stifle creative outlets and limit expanded thinking. By applying the light forces generated through crystals into personal practices and meditation, it is possible to dissolve the encrusted thought forms and patterns that create mental stagnation, emotional constriction, and physical dis-ease.

Crystal Healing

There have been many times in the course of human history when the mass populace based the foundation of their reality upon an untruth. As a race, people used to hold the common belief that the world was flat. It was generally accepted that the earth was the center of the universe and that the sun (as well as all of the stars) revolved around the earth. These concepts of reality dominated the minds of humans for centuries until they were disproved by the courageous individuals who dared to set themselves apart and go against the common thinking standards of the day to see reality with a clearer perspective. Even with proof it was difficult for the masses to alter their belief systems to accommodate a higher truth and a greater reality about the nature of life. Part of the difficulty in this type of mental change (as well as in changing our personal belief systems) is that we usually are more willing to accept ideas that somehow glorify our own personal sense of identity. The truth is oftentimes very humbling. To accept that the earth was not the center of the universe but instead a small planet on the far outskirts of the mother galaxy, or to accept that our personal ego sense of self will cease to exist with our last breath, is oftentimes a hard perspective to accommodate.

Today the group mind is still dominated by many outdated belief systems that shadow and cloud the light of truth. One of these concepts is that the soul is bound to the earth through sin. This breeds an innate sense of fear and guilt which is one of the most powerful controlling and manipulating techniques of dogmatic religions. Another concept that we have bought into is that we have many limitations in terms of healing ourselves of medically diagnosed incurable or terminal diseases. The acceptance of the belief that it is impossible to heal ourselves allows that thought to become the reality. Our susceptibility to the overviews that condition our minds can have such tremendous depowering effects as to render us helpless in circumstances that otherwise could serve as challenges and growth-producing situations.

One of the most destructive of all of the concepts that we have inherited is the sense of separatism. We see nations, peoples, cultures, countries and individuals as all being separate from one another. We see ourselves as being separate from extra-terrestrial forces and the earth as being separate from the rest of the universe. The bottom line is the lonely sense of separateness that we feel from ourselves and from a conscious connection with our own source of light. As we begin to identify with the light that is the common denominator in all manifest and unmanifest creation, we will come to the realization that in reality there is nothing that is separate from anything else. We will experience the sense of Oneness that comes from seeing the same light reflected in all seemingly individual forms. This will enable us to release the sense of separateness and create a world that has no boundaries or limitations in the expression of love, a world that is consciously unified in the light which comprises all being.

ORIGINS

The most commonly accepted creation perspective used to be the Christian theory that God created the world and everything in it in seven days. This overview was greatly replaced when Darwin's theory of evolution arrived on the scene. Even now that concept is gradually being replaced by the idea suggesting that we were bred and indeed programmed by higher life forms that visited our earth millions of years ago. This thought seems to be growing in the minds and hearts of men and women everywhere who somehow sense that we have a much grander conception within the vast expanse of the stars.

The belief that the human race has its origin in the heavens and that a divine inheritance is inevitable from foreparents of a highly advanced and evolved species is growing everyday. Let's open our minds to the possibility that our celestial ancestors originated in the sixth dimension close to the center of the great central sun at the core of our galaxy. Imagine that long ago they mastered the laws of time and space travel and spread their seed far out into the stars and the worlds that revolved around them; out as far as to reach a small star called the sun; out as far as the earth. They could have used Sirius as a transfer point into the third dimension and Venus as a gateway into our solar system. Visualize the potential that you have right now to consciously communicate through your thoughts with them. See yourself creating a bridge of light and love from our earth now existing in third dimensional reality, very far from the source of light of the great central sun, to connect with the beings that at this very moment await your thoughts in the sixth dimension. See the bridge of light connecting you with them and aligning everyone to the source at the center, creating one unified consciousness throughout all realms, dimensions, and planes of existence.

The reality is that reality is what we believe it to be. Let's be creative, let's have fun, let's use our imagination and creativity, expand our thoughts and concepts to include the unimaginable and the inconceivable. The ultimate truth will be even greater and stranger still.

As the mind shifts begin to occur, it will be possible for us to be consciously aware of interstellar vibrations (and beings) and integrate higher and more refined frequencies into our subtle bodies to manifest in undreamed-of physical realities. Working with the Master Crystals can facilitate this process of inter-dimensional communication and open the doors to perspectives that more fully accommodate our human potential.

ALTERATIONS

In the process of evolving consciousness, we learn from our experiences. It has become time when only the personal experience of the soul and of "God" will do. The age of believing has given birth to the Golden Age of knowing. Only our own unique individual experiences will serve to enlighten the illusions that bind our consciousness to earth plane ignorance.

The time has come when it is the responsibility of each individual entity on this planet to dedicate themselves to the process of initiating those experiences within oneself. It is now time to dedicate time and space to sit alone with yourself and experience the true sense of "beingness." It is time to close your eyes and look within and see who you really are, not the names and identities that you have known yourself to be all of your life, but the deepest, truest, purest essence of your self.

It is now possible, the energies are right, to tap into the source of infinity within ourselves—to claim it, to identify with it, to embrace, encompass and manifest it in our lives. It has taken the human being thousands of years and hundreds of lifetimes to be prepared for such a remarkable transformative experience. It is possible for each and every person.

It will take a bit of effort and a little courage to look beyond the personal identifications that have given us security all of our lives. It will require a sincerity and a conscious choice to release the grudges, sorrows, jealousies, guilts and pain that burden the heart. Most of all, what is needed is the willingness to let go of all that was in order to allow all that is to unfold. Trust and faith are required to dive into the black hole of the deepest fear within your heart and mind, to know that you will enter into the white light on the other side of it. The time is now. It is possible in this very moment.

Never before in the course of human history was the way made so open for so many to expand their consciousness to encompass the reality of their own being. As each individual commits and dedicates themselves to this process, the energy will increase and the way will be made easier for all those who will follow. It will be like the hundredth monkey effect, and people all over the world who have not been blessed with the freedoms and the environments to grow that we have will begin to "get it." As the process unfolds it will be as if we are waking from a deep unconscious sleep and we will begin to see life in a completely different way. As we unfold unto ourselves, we will come to see that the light we honor within ourselves is shining in the eyes of others. The love will flow and the peace will grow and the world will vibrate at a higher frequency, and the dream, the vision, that we all share deep within the core of our hearts will become the living reality. We shall become ONE, uniquely individual, but all plugged into the same source, all reflecting the same light, in a myriad of ways, in an infinite variety of colors.

We have been blessed with the freedom of choice, the opportunity to decide which way to go. This very individualized freedom is the most vital force that each one of us has at our disposal to contribute towards world peace. Let's individually decide that we will learn to be at peace with ourselves and that we will no longer contribute to antagonistic thoughts or feelings or conversations or actions. Instead, choose peace, choose love. Make the choice. It is your divine right. It is that choice that will plug you right into the divine source. It will plug you into such a power and a purpose that will direct your life and give you more meaning than you can imagine. The choice is yours. It is mine. It is for us to choose our destinies and the ultimate history of this planet. We are the creators here. We have been endowed with the most precious gift in the universe: to choose. To choose peace over conflict, love over jealousy, forgiveness over anger, understanding over guilt, joy over sorrow, and happiness over discontent. Make your choice now and affirm it with every breath you take. Put it into action and receive your divine heritage. Plug into the infinite source of light within you and be who you really are, and manifest your world the way you envision it to be.

ADVANCEMENTS

Somewhere in the faint hint of our genetic memory lies the knowledge of the universe and worlds where life is free from the illusion of time and space. Just as it has been programmed into us to reawaken at the perfect moment, it now invites our attention. We have a purpose far greater than we might have ever imagined. It seeks our acknowledgment now and asks that we cut the circuits to the thought patterns and futile emotions that keep us bound to the illusion and the confusion of the lower mental realms. Release, let go, align, and come into the reality of true being that will give you inner peace. The time is upon us and the hour is now to awaken to the truth of our own identity that is written within the depths of our genes. We are all of the same spirit, and that spirit is the uniting force that can and will transform the very nature of the earth if we but surrender to it. There is so much more that awaits us, so much more that is in the realm of possibility once we unite our integrated spirits into a common cause. Our solar system is but our back yard, the Milky Way Galaxy our neighborhood and the physical plane our schooling. Let's travel!! Let's claim our heritage and build our sweet earth the garden that she deserves and then expand from that home base to outreach further than we can now even conceive of. It starts with willingness, then effort and determination, and concludes with success.

Use your crystals to align your consciousness to the cosmic harmony that they exemplify. Work with them and let them work for you. Allow their light forces to clear your aura so that you can manifest into your life what it is that you require to fulfill your greatest potential and destiny. Crystal power is in abundance now to serve you and integrate your individual identity with that of a much greater whole.

There is a powerful light force that is moving towards our planet as the entity of earth seeks to align herself with the great central sun at the center of our galaxy. As the frequencies raise in vibration, every living thing will be affected. Nothing will be left untouched. There are extraterrestrial and discarnate forces that are monitoring and assisting in the assimilation of this light force into the hearts and minds of people everywhere. The ability to let go of outdated beliefs and old programming that no longer serve this light is the key to merging with the forces at hand. Those who are unwilling to set aside ego structures that only serve their personal purpose will have a very difficult time during this period as the influx of energy increases. These people will need extra support and prayers during these times.

It is a time of personal responsibility. It is a time of courage—to face our own fears and to slay our own dragons of darkness. It is a time to support one another in that process and to rekindle the spirit of love into each and every relationship, beginning with ourself, for ourself. It is a time when the rainbow ray of light can be utilized by each individual. Every facet, every chakra, every aspect of our lives can come into balance if we surrender in the deepest, most sacred part of our hearts to the light. Allow it to come in, identify with it. It is you, it is me, it is us, it is all there is.

PEACE

So often our minds become constricted in the narrow focus of our lives and the events upon this earth which can create such a great effect on us. It is as if we devote our precious creative energy in affirming the reality that has been programmed into our consciousness by other sources. In this tunnel vision the world and life often appear in shades of doom and gloom, which are perpetuated and made even stronger by our thoughts accepting it.

Let's imagine for a moment that life isn't made of war and peoples and nations at odds with one another. Let's instead paint a different picture altogether and put our creative energy into that. We have all the paints and an infinite number of colors at our disposal. What shall we create? How would you choose it to be—personally, interpersonally, socially, communally, nationally and planetarily? Let's combine our thoughts together to strengthen the creative force. As you read this, link with the collective mind of the thousands of people that will also read this, and imagine peace. Pure peace . . . within ourselves first. This means that any of those old grudges or jealousies or hurts, guilts, sorrows, fears, or pains, must be released. Exhale them now, and with the following inhale take your personal image of peace into the center core of your heart, and again exhale and let go of anything within you that is prohibiting your complete experience of personal peace. Allow yourself to come into alignment with your own divine source of peace and power and love, and give it to yourself first. Feel it, create it, become it.

Now expand that sense of peace into your thoughts about the people that you are closest to, and let go of any friction that may be existing between you. Again exhale and let go. Inhale and envision each person you love (and want to love) surrounded in the peace that you feel. Expand the thought to include everyone in your town. (Those of you who live in big cities, increase the voltage!) And now, the nation, and the world. Expand the vision and see our earth existing in a state of peace with the moon, the other planets of our solar system, and with the sun. Grab onto one of your favorite crystals and let this beam of peace connect you to the center core of the galaxy and with the great central sun, which emanates light, life, and love throughout our universe. Be there in the center for a moment and feel who you are outside of your physical existence here on earth. Align your soul to the great cosmic forces that created your being.

Now from this perspective view your life here on earth. Is it really so serious? Do all those little things really matter so much? Is your personal balance dependent on the constant changes existing on this planet? No. You have the choice at every moment to choose peace, to choose love, to choose alignment, and to choose to channel the light available to you.

Now just take a moment to join minds and hearts with someone else who at this very moment is also focusing on the light. Let's brighten the force. Let's create a chain reaction so strong that anything less than this light will be encompassed by it and the darker energies will be dissolved in its brilliance. Link your light with all of the souls, carnate or discarnate, earthly or extra-terrestrial, that are dedicated to the expansion and expression of light.

When you feel down or feel the emotional waves about ready to engulf you, call upon the light within you. Evoke it! Ask its presence to come forth and assist you. Identify with it, and channel it to bring balance and order into each situation. It is the most transformative force in the universe and one that will never fail you.

Let's give to the earth the heritage that she deserves. Let's use our alchemical powers and transform her back into the garden, back to the pure thought of peace and harmony. Are you ready? Let's go for it!! We can do it!!

*   *   *

It is almost dawn and the sun is about to rise over the sacred Taos Mountain as the first hints of gold and red appear on the eastern horizon. And it is time that I end this chapter and this book, even though there is more to share. It will have to wait until Volume III. I sense that this is enough for now, and when it has been digested there will be more for all of us to assimilate. May the information contained within the pages of this book serve your personal, inter-personal, professional, and planetary purpose.

WITH LOVE.

ACKNOWLEDGMENTS

Linda Bauer	Love, Understanding and Typing
Stephen Bradley	Photographs-Stone Layouts & Katrina
Andrea Cagan	Assistance in Channeling Master Crystal Information
Gary Fleck	Earthkeeper Model & Numerology Consultation
Lafe Harrower	Model for Layouts
Ingrid Rameau	Numerology Consultation
Duane and Twila Mattsson	Unconditional Love and Support
Orion, Serenelle and the Gang	For "Being There"
Sananda Ra	Support, Encouragement, Inspiration
Simran	For sharing his Mother with the World
Barbara Somerfield	Continued Support, Editing, Publication
Lee Valkenaar	Earthkeeper Photograph

SNEAK PREVIEW
OF VOLUME III

The use of crystals for protection against nuclear radiation
The remaining six Master Crystals
Inner earth beings emerging?!
Advanced techniques in Laser Wand surgery

THE CRYSTAL ACADEMY

THE CRYSTAL ACADEMY OF ADVANCED HEAL-
ING ARTS, located in Taos, New Mexico, is now open
to facilitate further education in the art, theory and practice of Crystal Healing (see address below).

FOR FURTHER INFORMATION

Quartz Crystals, beginning, intermediate and advanced
sets of healing stones, smudge sticks and information on
classes and workshops can also be obtained by sending a
self addressed stamped envelope to:
Crystal Enlightenment
P. O. Box 3208
Taos, New Mexico 87571

CRYSTAL ENLIGHTENMENT
The Transforming Properties of Crystals and Healing Stones

Katrina Raphaell

This book is a comprehensive, yet easy to understand guide to the use of crystals and gems for internal growth, healing and balance in your daily life. Discover new resources, learn how to extend your personal awareness and center by attuning to crystal energies. The magnitude and potential of crystals and gems to impact positively our personal lives and the evolving planet we live on is significant.

Some of the topics explored in this book are:
• What are crystals physically and esoterically?
• Working with crystals for self-healing
• The ancient art of laying on stones
• Psychic Protection
• Generator Crystals
• Important healing stones and their uses
• Double terminated stones and their functions
• Crystal Meditations
• Black Holes

Crystal Enlightenment is designed for the lay person, as well as the professional, to give the basic understanding necessary to use the healing properties inherent within the mineral kingdom to improve the quality of our external and internal lives.

ISBN: 0-943358-27-2   Paperback   5½ x 8½   175 Pages $9.95

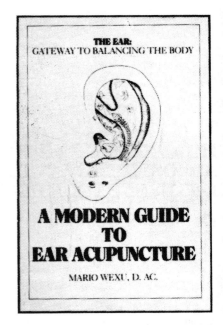

THE EAR: GATEWAY TO BALANCING THE BODY

A MODERN GUIDE TO EAR ACUPUNCTURE

Mario Wexu, D.AC

This is the first comprehensive modern textbook of ear acupuncture. The author uniquely combines his extensive personal clinical experience with traditional and modern Chinese and European sources. Anatomical descriptions with detailed charts clearly illustrate how to locate and use over three hundred ear points, both alone and in combination with body points, to treat and prevent illness. Case histories with specific techniques cover problems such as:

- Deafness
- Otitis
- Otalgia
- Drug Addiction
- Tobacco Addiction
- Alcoholism
- Obesity
- Anesthesia
- Oedema
- Insomnia
- Acupuncture Anesthesia
- Electronic Acupuncture Devices

An excellent repertory listing 130 diseases facilitates an understanding of this incredible and valuable healing art.

ISBN: 0-943358-08-6   Paperback   6 × 9   217 Pages $12.50

HOW COSMIC AND ATMOSPHERIC ENERGIES INFLUENCE YOUR HEALTH

Dr. Michel Gauquelin

The first and only comprehensive research on how atmospheric conditions, rhythms of nature and cosmic cycles affect mental, psychological and physical health. Summer, autumn, winter, spring—each season brings its own risks. Deaths are more frequent when a weather front passes over, fogs can kill. Sudden drops in barometric pressure, synthetic clothing, building materials, designs and electrical agitation in the air affect the complex balance of health and disease.

Dangers to health are intensified by pollution of the home, work and earth environment. Learn about your mental and physical vulnerabilities and reactions to atmospheric conditions and the personal effects of cosmic influences such as sunspots and lunar cycles.

Therapeutic indications are explained to help you deal with stressful environmental conditions that influence your life and well-being.

Dr. Michel Gauquelin, is a leading international researcher, psychologist and statistician. Since 1969 he has been the director of the Laboratory for the Study of the Relationship Between Cosmic and Psycho-Physiological Rhythms in Paris, France.

ISBN: 0-943358-14-0   **Paperback**   5½ × 8½   **188 Pages**   **$8.95**

SILVER DENTAL FILLINGS THE TOXIC TIMEBOMB
Can The Mercury In Your Dental Fillings Poison You?

Sam Ziff

A significant and shocking expose of one of the greatest health dangers of our time. The amalgam used to fill teeth is 40 to 50 per cent mercury, a known poison. This book explains how mercury migrates from the teeth into the body affecting our overall health in a dramatic manner. This groundbreaking book includes the following topics and questions:

- Mercury in Medicine and Dentistry
- The History of Mercury in Medicine
- The Arguments For and Against
- Do we really have electricity in our mouths?
- Measurement of Mercury in the urine
- How long does it stay in the body?
- Mercury in the body, where does it go?
- Does Mercury cause any changes in our tissues and organs?
- Does Mercury cause psychiatric and behavioral changes?
- Micromercurialism, signs and symptoms

This pioneering book is written in a clear straightforward manner, ideal for the layman and professional who want to become aware of the body of information currently available on mercury toxicity from dental amalgams. Then, informed, each individual can draw his own conclusions.

"Silver Dental Fillings alerts the reader to the need for more research and understanding of the role that mercury amalgam may have on chronic health dysfunction."   **JEFFREY BLAND, Ph.D.**

THE PULSE
IN OCCIDENT AND ORIENT
Its Philosophy And Practice
In Holistic Diagnosis And Treatment

The most significant diagnostic technique available to the medical profession has always been the pulse. This unprecedented text presents a detailed examination of the possible interpretations of this simple indication of the presence of life, from the point of view of four major medical traditions. Included is the historical background, detailed analysis and descriptions of the diagnostic uses of the pulse in Iran, China, India and the West.

This comprehensive text describes:

- Chinese Healing Precepts
- Ayurvedic Philosophy & The Pulse
- Technique Of Taking The Pulse
- Dreams & The Pulse
- The Pregnancy Pulse

- The Pulse & Organ Relationships
- Arabian Medicine & The Pulse
- Diseases & The Pulse
- Seasons & The Pulse
- The Death Pulse

The Pulse In Occident and Orient is a significant and unparalleled compliation of the similarities and differences in pulse diagnosis in different cultures and its current relevance as an important tool in holistic diagnosis and treatment.

ISBN: 0-943358-29-9   Paperback   6 x 9   232 Pages $12.50

TAOIST SECRETS OF LOVE
Cultivating Male Sexual Energy

Mantak Chia • Michael Winn

Master Mantak Chia reveals for the first time to the general public, the ancient sexual secrets of the Taoist sages. These secrets enable men to conserve and transform sexual energy through its circulation in the Microcosmic Orbit, invigorating and rejuvenating the body's vital functions. Hidden for centuries, these esoteric techniques and principles, make the process of linking sexual energy and transcendent states of consciousness accessible to the reader.

This revolutionary and definitive book teaches:
• Higher Taoist practices for alchemical transmutation of body, mind and spirit
• The secret of achieving and maintaining full sexual potency
• The Taoist "valley orgasm"—Pathway to higher bliss
• How to conserve and store sperm in the body
• The exchange and balancing of male and female energies, within the body and with one's partner
• How this practice can fuel higher achievement in career and sports

Taoist Secrets of Love is not just another flowery philosophical treatise on the ecstasies of oriental love. It is a pragmatic handbook that distills the secret teachings on sex of four living Taoist masters sought out by Mantak Chia during fifteen years of travel and study in the Far East. The Taoist practice of chi cultivation focuses on integrating the divine or subtle energies into the human body, with the goal of achieving a dynamic balance of opposing energies called Yin and Yang. The Tao is the indescribable sum and absolute source of these energies, which manifest in ever changing form. The Taoists, being practical, proposed that a man can begin with the most accessible energy at hand, the sexual attraction between men and women, and use that force as a springboard to more subtle realms."—**MICHAEL WINN**

Michael Winn has travelled to sixty countries as a journalist, photographer, expedition guide and observer of global culture.

ISBN: 0-943358-19-1   Paperback   6 × 9   215 Pages